W9-AEK-902

THEME STUDIES

BUTTERFLIES ABOUND!

A WHOLE LANGUAGE RESOURCE GUIDE FOR K–4

Seddon Kelly Beaty   Irene Fountas

ADDISON WESLEY LONGMAN, INC.

Menlo Park, California • Reading, Massachusetts • New York
Don Mills, Ontario • Wokingham, England • Amsterdam • Bonn • Sydney
Singapore • Tokyo • Madrid • San Juan • Paris • Seoul, Korea
Milan • Mexico City • Taipei, Taiwan

This book is a publication of Addison Wesley Longman, Inc.

Managing Editor: Diane Silver

Project Editor: Rachel Farber

Content Editor: Elly Schotman

Production Manager: Janet Yearian

Production Coordinator: Barbara Atmore

Design Manager: Jeff Kelly

Cover and text design: Square Moon Productions

Cover illustration: Elizabeth Morales-Denny

Text illustrations: Rachel Gage

ISBN: 0-201-45504-8

4 5 6 7 8 9 10–ML–00 99 98 97 96

CONTENTS

Concept 1:   INSECTS 4
              Butterflies belong to a group of animals called insects.

Concept 2:   METAMORPHOSIS and ANATOMY 9
              During its lifetime, a butterfly passes through four stages. This process is called metamorphosis. The four stages are: egg, caterpillar (larva), chrysalis (pupa), butterfly. Each stage looks very different and has its own distinct anatomy.

Concept 3:   BASIC NEEDS and BEHAVIORS 33
              Each stage of a butterfly (egg, caterpillar, chrysalis, and butterfly) needs certain conditions in order to develop. Each stage has survival behaviors and adaptations that help it meet the challenges of its environment.

Concept 4:   PROTECTIVE BEHAVIORS 47
              Each stage of a butterfly (egg, caterpillar, chrysalis, and butterfly) has behaviors and adaptations that help it escape predators.

Concept 5:   VARIETY and CLASSIFICATION 52
              The eggs, caterpillars, chrysalises, and butterflies of different species display a great variety of colors, shapes, and sizes. Scientists classify butterflies into groups according to various attributes.

INTRODUCTION

Butterflies Abound is a teacher resource book for a theme study about butterflies. It is intended for use with children from kindergarten through grade four. A theme study is an open-ended, in-depth investigation of a topic. Students engage in learning experiences in various curriculum areas. They use and develop the strategies and skills of the different disciplines as they raise and investigate questions, solve problems, and share their acquired knowledge.

To begin the *Butterflies Abound* theme study, you and your students will need to acquire at least one classroom caterpillar or chrysalis. As students observe and discuss the different stages of the developing butterfly, background knowledge will be pooled and scientific questions will be raised:

> What kind of caterpillar is it?
>
> Which end is its head?
>
> Why isn't it moving?
>
> When will it become a butterfly?

The particular questions your students ask will determine the content and direction of their butterfly theme study. This resource book contains a vast array of learning experiences that will help you provide opportunities for your students to explore and find answers to the questions they have raised.

Children view their world as a whole and explore it every way they can, without labeling and separating their learning processes into separate subject areas. A theme study reflects this natural, integrated approach to learning. For convenience, the learning experiences in *Butterflies Abound* have been organized into nine subject areas: **Science, Language Arts, Math, Social Studies, Art, Dramatic Play, Music, Physical Activities,** and **Cooking.** This is an artificial division; all the suggested learning experiences cross subject areas and involve a variety of processes. However, we feel that this organization makes the Guide easier to use as a resource, and helps teachers who are new to a theme study approach realize the wide range of possible learning experiences.

The *Butterflies Abound* theme study begins with the students' scientific observations and queries about caterpillars, chrysalises, and butterflies. Consequently, the **Science** section is the starting point and the core of this Guide. It is divided into five scientific concepts or subtopics about butterflies.

Concept 1: INSECTS
Butterflies belong to a group of animals called insects.

Concept 2: METAMORPHOSIS and ANATOMY
During its lifetime, a butterfly passes through four stages. This process is called metamorphosis. The four stages are: egg, caterpillar (larva), chrysalis (pupa), butterfly. Each stage looks very different and has its own distinct anatomy.

Concept 3: BASIC NEEDS and BEHAVIORS
Each stage of a butterfly (egg, caterpillar, chrysalis, and butterfly) needs certain conditions in order to develop. Each stage has survival behaviors and adaptations that help it meet the challenges of its environment.

Concept 4: PROTECTIVE BEHAVIORS
Each stage of a butterfly (egg, caterpillar, chrysalis, and butterfly) has behaviors and adaptations that help it escape predators.

Concept 5: VARIETY and CLASSIFICATION
The eggs, caterpillars, chrysalises, and butterflies of different species display a great variety of colors, shapes, and sizes. Scientists classify butterflies into groups according to various attributes.

For each science concept, we have:

- included some questions children often ask that could prompt exploration into that subtopic

- provided relevant scientific background information for the teacher

- suggested learning experiences to help students explore their questions and develop understandings. Related experiences offered in the other eight subject area sections: **Language Arts, Math, Social Studies, Art, Dramatic Play, Music, Physical Activities,** and **Cooking** are cross-referenced here.

The *Butterflies Abound* Experiences Web on the following page presents an overview of the organization of this Guide and a sampling of the learning experiences offered in each curriculum area. Every butterfly theme study will include a broad range of these interdisciplinary experiences; however, the particular experiences in each theme study will be determined and shaped by the questions, interests, and input of the students. The "Sample Butterfly Inquiry: From Questions to Experiences" on pages xxii–xxiii presents an illustration of this process, based on the theme study with one particular group of students.

Experiences Web

MATH

Count and estimate butterflies in a natural habitat
Measure and chart caterpillar food consumption
Measure and graph caterpillar growth and butterfly wing span
Record the length of each stage in butterfly life cycle
Explore caterpillar color patterns and symmetrical butterfly wing patterns
Create realistic and fanciful butterfly drawings on the computer

SOCIAL STUDIES

Read and create maps showing ranges of different butterflies
Read butterfly legends and tales from different cultures
Learn about the history of butterflies
Discuss and participate in butterfly conservation efforts
Learn about butterfly gardening

LANGUAGE ARTS

Enjoy butterfly finger plays, poems, and chants
Experiment with oral reading, in unison and in parts
Tape record solo and group readings of favorite pieces
Read, listen to, and discuss books
Dramatize books through Readers Theatre and informal adaptations
Participate in Big Book shared readings
Explore print through Big Book experiences
Innovate to create new versions of predictable songs, poems, and stories
Create charts and diagrams
Write poems, stories, reports, letters, labels, signs
Write and illustrate individual and class books

SCIENCE

Observe developing classroom butterfly
Participate in caring for butterfly
Describe and chart features and behaviors
Pose questions about the developing butterfly
Make observational drawings
Write in butterfly journals, learning logs, etc.
Record information on life cycle charts
Read books about butterfly metamorphosis and anatomy
Learn about butterfly needs and protective behaviors

SCIENCE

Examine anatomical charts
Look at butterfly wing scales with microscope
Dramatize butterfly life cycle
Learn about how butterflies feed, reproduce, and overwinter
Look at butterfly field guides; discuss different species
Classify butterfly pictures according to attributes
Prepare and present reports about specific butterflies
Visit local butterfly habitats, insect collections, and butterfly zoos
Classify characteristics of insects

DRAMATIC PLAY

Use puppets, felt-board characters, and props to act out stories and/or life cycle
Prepare and present plays, skits, and shared reading performances
Create dramatic play environments: insect museum, butterfly habitat

PHYSICAL ACTIVITIES

Play games reinforcing butterfly concepts: Butterfly Camouflage Tag, Metamorphosis Obstacle Course, etc.
Imitate caterpillar and butterfly movements

COOKING

Follow simple recipes to create snacks for a butterfly celebration

ART

Create realistic and fanciful caterpillar, butterfly, and life cycle art, inspired by observation and experiences
Explore different art forms and media: drawing, painting, collage, printing, sculpting, mobiles, etc.

MUSIC

Sing songs
Create new verses
Add rhythm, movement, and instruments to songs
Make sing-along books, illustrating the words of the song
Tape record singing for later listening

A STATEMENT OF OUR BELIEFS ABOUT LEARNING AND TEACHING

Whole-Language Beliefs

Based on a whole-language philosophy, there are several underlying beliefs about learning and teaching that have guided us in the development of the *Butterflies Abound* Resource Guide.

* All students are capable of learning. They come to school with varied background knowledge, strengths, and learning needs. As they explore a topic, they learn in different ways. For example, a child may learn about a butterfly's anatomy through creating an observational drawing, through listening to or reading a book, or through singing a song. A wide variety of learning experiences helps students build an effective repertoire of skills and strategies.

* Children learn by being immersed in what they are learning. Thus, in this Guide we suggest that students be surrounded by and involved with butterfly artifacts, books, and experiences: raising butterflies, drawing, reading, writing, talking, and singing about butterflies.

* Children are motivated to learn when they are actively involved in pursuing their own needs and interests, and finding answers to their own questions. Learning becomes purposeful and relevant.

Thus we believe the direction of the butterfly inquiry should be guided by the students' interests and questions. With the guidance of the teacher, the students should make many of the decisions about what to learn and how to learn about butterflies.

* Children learn how to learn by watching the learning process being demonstrated, and by participating with the teacher. Throughout this Guide, teachers have opportunities to demonstrate ways to learn about butterflies, modeling such processes as: observing the caterpillar closely; asking questions; locating and reading a section of a text that answers a specific question; developing a report form; using a hand lens to examine a butterfly; using cloze techniques to figure out an unfamiliar word, etc.

* Children need time to learn and time to practice or use what they have learned in meaningful contexts. For example, students learn to write through writing labels, creating charts, or writing poems or reports.

* Children need feedback to help them assess their learning and to guide further attempts. As the children brainstorm and discuss their ideas, create charts, read Readers Theatre scripts, and share their writing, they receive responses from their teacher and peers. Talking and sharing are

vital steps in developing concepts and producing creative, reflective work. Therefore, discussions and cooperative learning are important facets of most of the learning experiences suggested in this Guide.

The Inquiry Process

In a classroom where the inquiry process is valued, students are motivated by their own curiosity. In this way, they gain control of their own learning, contributing to its direction and feeling rewarded by the process. Students pose questions, identify areas of interest, and plan their approach to a problem. They gather materials, and then collect, record, discuss, and compare information. New knowledge stimulates new questions, and the inquiry process continues. Students are continually challenged to figure out new ways to learn. They use a wide variety of resources to solve problems and build their pool of knowledge. Their teacher demonstrates, facilitates, coaches, confirms, and contributes to the process.

In the following pages we describe some of the ways our classes have used the inquiry process to pursue the butterfly theme study. A model of the process is shown below.

A Model of the Inquiry Process

Brainstorm

Prior Knowledge → Questions

Organize by Subtopic

Decide What Questions to Pursue

Brainstorm and Model Ways to Research Sample Questions

Decide Who Will Assume Responsibility for Questions
(large group, small group, partners, individuals)

Class Contributes Resources to Each Other

Gather and Organize Information

Teacher Facilitates Inquiry Process

Share Information with Others

BEGINNING THE INQUIRY

At the start of the theme study, it is important for you to find out what your students know in order to build on their previous knowledge and to discover misconceptions. One way to begin is to simply ask, "What do you know about butterflies?" You or the students can record the information on a large chart. As children share what they think they know, listen carefully to develop an understanding of each individual's and the group's knowledge. It is important to understand what the children know in order to develop ideas on how to link their existing understanding with new understandings.

What We Know About Butterflies

They like flowers.

They once were caterpillars.

They have wings.

They have antennae.

They are fragile.

They lay eggs.

Another way to record this preliminary information is to create a web of all the ideas. Initially the ideas can be written randomly around the major topic: butterflies. Misconceptions and varying opinions should also be listed because they provide wonderful opportunities for discussing, revising, and providing evidence for one's thinking during the study.

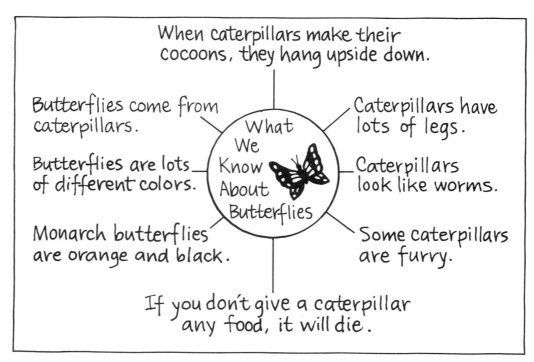

When caterpillars make their cocoons, they hang upside down.

Butterflies come from caterpillars.

Caterpillars have lots of legs.

Butterflies are lots of different colors.

Caterpillars look like worms.

What We Know About Butterflies

Monarch butterflies are orange and black.

Some caterpillars are furry.

If you don't give a caterpillar any food, it will die.

Later the class can come back to the web and reorganize their ideas as subtopics, adding any new information that is offered. Examples of information added during this process are shown in parentheses in the web below. The teacher will need to assist in this process by asking questions such as, "Can anyone think of a name for this group of ideas?" or "In which group should we put this information?"

What We Know - Random Brainstorm Organized

What They Look Like
Caterpillars look like worms.
Caterpillars have lots of legs.
(Butterflies have four wings.)
(Butterflies have a curled-up proboscis.)

How They Stay Alive
If you don't give a caterpillar any food, it will die.
(Caterpillars eat leaves.)
(Some butterflies fly south in the winter.)

Butterflies

Life Cycle
Butterflies come from caterpillars.
When caterpillars make their cocoons, they hang upside down.
(Butterflies lay eggs.)

Different Kinds of Butterflies
Butterflies are lots of different colors.
Monarch butterflies are orange and black.
(Swallowtail butterflies have fancy-shaped wings.)

After the students have shared what they know about butterflies, elicit a series of questions. It is important to discover your students' particular curiosities and interests in order to establish a meaningful initial focus for the theme study. Ask questions such as these:

What do you want to find out about butterflies?

What do you want to learn about?

What are you curious about?

Record the questions generated by the group on chart paper. A sample chart, "What We Want to Know About Butterflies," is provided below. To encourage the students to expand their questions, you may want to prompt other related queries. For example you might say, *John has asked if butterflies live at the North Pole. Do you have any other questions about where butterflies live?* You should also feel free to share your own genuine questions about butterflies, both to demonstrate good questions and to show that this inquiry will be a problem-solving process for all.

What We Want to Know About Butterflies

May 10 How does a caterpillar turn into a butterfly?
Can we keep the caterpillar?
What does our caterpillar eat?
Do caterpillars bite people?

May 13 How many legs does our caterpillar have?
How big will our caterpillar get?
Can the caterpillar hear us?

May 16 How will the caterpillar know when it's time to become a chrysalis?
Can we keep the butterfly?

Next, help students organize the questions into groups or subtopics. Re-write the groups of related questions under appropriate heads on a question chart. A sample chart: "Our Butterfly Questions—Organized," is provided below.

Our Butterfly Questions-Organized

What Does a Caterpillar Look Like?
How many legs does our caterpillar have?
(How big will our caterpillar get?)

What Can a Caterpillar Do?
Do caterpillars bite people?
(Can the caterpillar hear us?)

How Does Metamorphosis Work?
How does a caterpillar turn into a butterfly?
(How will the caterpillar know when it's time
    to become a chrysalis?)

What Does a Caterpillar Need to Stay Healthy?
Can we keep the caterpillar?
What does our caterpillar eat?

What Does a Butterfly Need to Stay Healthy?
(Can we keep the butterfly?)

As students become more deeply involved in their investigation and more knowledgeable about their topic, further questions will arise. Add these questions to the class chart(s). This ongoing process will help students develop the important understanding that one question often leads to another and that new learning fosters new questions. Brainstorming new questions can be done as a whole class or in small groups, or students can individually add questions to the class chart. The new questions should be dated and/or written on the list in a different color. Sometimes new questions will be added to existing groups on the organized question web. Sometimes a new heading will need to be established.

ORGANIZING THE INVESTIGATION

Once the theme study has been launched, the investigation will take many paths. Students will continue to share their interests and curiosities, and both you and the students will plan experiences to further the learning. The rich selection of experiences suggested in this Guide will engage students in a variety of processes across the curriculum and facilitate the inquiry process.

The learning experiences in the Guide can be explored by the whole class, by a small group of students interested in a particular subtopic, or by individual students. We encourage you to use a variety of groupings. We feel it is especially rewarding and meaningful to help students form groups according to their particular interests, to support these groups as they plan and pursue relevant learning experiences, and finally to help the groups find meaningful ways to share their new knowledge with the class. You will want to experiment with ways to adapt this process to suit the age, ability, and dynamics of your class. The following tips may be helpful in organizing diverse research groups:

* Refer to the organized class question chart. Have students select topics they would like to pursue at this point.

* Together, brainstorm additional questions for those topics and ways that students can try to find answers to the questions.

* Have each student choose one initial question to explore. Groups will be formed according to the chosen topic of interest.

As teacher, your key role in this learning process is that of a facilitator—steering the students in productive directions, assisting in the location of pertinent resources, modeling new relevant skills, and providing lots of encouragement. The "Sample Butterfly Inquiry: From Questions to Experience" provided on pages xxii–xxiii, provides a helpful model of how to use the *Butterflies Abound* Guide to locate appropriate learning experiences that will offer students the opportunity to explore and find answers to their particular questions.

If the Inquiry Process is a new approach for your class, it is particularly important that you demonstrate and talk the students through the steps of planning an approach, researching, organizing, and recording information. Skills such as taking notes, making a list, and organizing ideas into categories need to be modeled and practiced through whole-group learning experiences. Later, students will be able to engage in these processes more independently. Eventually students will be able to come up with their own organizational study plans. One plan outlined by a group of third grade students looked like this:

Question: Do butterflies live through the winter?

Researchers: Tom, Jean, Charlotte, Ari

Our Ways to Find and Record Information:

Tom: interview my neighbor, the science teacher

Jean: get books from the library to read with my group

Charlotte: record information for chart on index
cards as we read and discuss books

Ari: do writing and illustrating on our chart

All: think of questions to ask Tom's neighbor
and create a form for presenting information (a chart)

CONCLUDING THE INQUIRY

Toward the end of the theme study, encourage students to make a list of what they now know about butterflies. As they compare it to their original list or web, they will realize how their knowledge has grown. They can discuss the different ways they have gathered knowledge and note questions that remain unanswered.

To bring their study to a conclusion, the students can plan ways of sharing their new understandings with others. Sharing can take many forms. Some students have created schoolwide displays of their projects in the corridors, auditorium, or schoolyard. Some have created and organized classroom performances that include songs, poetry reading, skits, and artwork, and have invited families, librarians, and others who helped make the theme study a success. Others have simply created a classroom environment of projects completed during their study such as posters, published books, or an art display, and invited others to look at their work. One class cooperatively published a thematic newspaper filled with songs, poems, chants, book reports, factual articles, and photographs with captions.

Your students will undoubtedly think of lots of meaningful ways they would like to celebrate the culmination of their inquiry. Whatever the decision, it is important that students engage in the planning, arranging, and evaluating of their conclusion. They need to discuss what they feel is important to share (major ideas) and ways they want to share these ideas (posters, charts, songs, plays, live specimens). They also need to decide what work needs to be done and carry out those tasks—for example: creating a chart, preparing a display, giving a talk, publishing an informational book, editing and copying over a poem, preparing a guest list and a guest book, writing invitations, and preparing refreshments.

INITIATING YOUR BUTTERFLY THEME STUDY

Teacher Preparation

* Arrange to get at least one caterpillar or chrysalis. Order from the sources listed in Appendix C and/or try to find local caterpillars and chrysalises. If your students have observed and studied butterfly metamorphosis in previous years, you might want to consider hosting two species of butterflies for students to compare and contrast. Read "Obtaining Butterflies for Your Classroom" (page xix) for further information.

* Skim through this Guide. Familiarize yourself with its organization and contents so you are aware of the wide range of learning experiences suggested, and so you can consider some of the ways you might choose to respond to your students' questions and interests.

* Gather resources. Collect books, poems, magazine articles, and other butterfly materials listed in the Bibliography. Many of the poems we have enjoyed with our students are not reproduced in this Guide, but have been clearly referenced. We strongly encourage you to gather and share some of these excellent poems with your class. Collect butterfly pictures and artifacts. Enrich your theme study by contacting local butterfly experts and enthusiasts and by taking advantage of local resources. For example, an entomologist may be willing to make a classroom presentation; a naturalist may be willing to lead a field trip to a local area rich in butterflies; or a curator may be willing to guide your class through the insect collection at a local museum.

* Write some of the poems, chants, and song words on large chart paper for use in shared reading warm-ups and independent student enjoyment. See the Language Arts (Fingerplays, Poems, and Chants) and Music sections.

* Plan some introductory experiences to engage the students. We often find it useful to start the day with a warm-up of finger plays, chants, po-

ems, and songs related to the butterfly study. This shared reading sets a mood of community, enjoyment, participation, and focused creative energy. Fiction and nonfiction books can be read aloud and followed by creative art, drama, science, and/or writing experiences.

* Set up a Butterfly Observation Center in your classroom. Establish the center in a place that students can choose to visit independently and in small groups at many times during the day. Some of the most meaningful learning takes place through this type of unscheduled, child-initiated observation. Establish some simple rules to ensure the safety and well-being of the insect. You may wish to equip your butterfly center with: hand lenses; string and rulers for measuring; writing and drawing materials; reproducible Observation Sheets (provided in Appendix A); and a class chart on which students can write questions, respond to other questions, and draw or describe caterpillar or butterfly behaviors they have seen. A classroom Butterfly Research Center with books and posters can be located nearby.

Obtaining Butterflies for Your Classroom

The investigation of butterflies will begin when an egg, caterpillar, chrysalis, or adult butterfly arrives in your classroom. It is important that the children raise their own butterflies so they can observe the life cycle changes first-hand. The experience is fascinating and memorable, giving students a real motivation to learn more about butterflies, and rooting the new knowledge in a meaningful context.

Commercially available "butterfly kits" are relatively inexpensive and extremely easy to use. The Butterfly Garden is the most widely available kit. It includes three to five Painted Lady caterpillars. The tiny caterpillars arrive in a plastic container with all necessary food provided. When they are ready to become chrysalises, the caterpillars hang from the paper-lined lid of the container. After the chrysalises are formed, the paper liner is removed from the lid and taped to the inside of a cardboard and acetate butterfly cage. The length of time from the purchase of the caterpillars to the release of the adult butterflies is about three weeks.

Various swallowtail butterflies and Monarchs are also commercially available. They are usually sold as chrysalises. The butterfly hatches from the chrysalis approximately one to two weeks after it is purchased. Addresses of companies selling a variety of caterpillars and chrysalises are provided in Appendix C.

Caterpillars, chrysalises, and butterfly eggs can also be found outside and brought into the classroom. Concept 3: Basic Needs in the Science section provides suggestions for finding, housing and caring for the developing insect, and suggests additional resource books.

It is best to schedule a butterfly theme study at a time of year when the adult butterflies can be released to fly free. For butterflies to thrive, the outside temperature should generally be 60° Fahrenheit, or warmer. Therefore, in northern climates, late spring, summer, and early fall are the best seasons. Monarch caterpillars and chrysalises can brought into the classroom in the early fall. When released, the classroom Monarch will join the other members of its species, migrating south for the winter.

USING THE *BUTTERFLIES ABOUND* GUIDE

Adapting the Guide to Answer Your Students' Questions

Your students' questions and interests will determine the direction of their butterfly theme study, the specific selection of learning experiences, and the length of time spent in the investigation. Each theme study will be unique because it will be shaped by the students and teacher of a particular class. This Guide, therefore, has no prescribed sequence. The five Science concepts can be explored in any order, depending on the specific questions your students raise. Often several concepts will be explored simultaneously.

For example, the children will probably pose many questions about the appearance and behavior of the classroom caterpillar. Many of these questions can be answered through the experiences provided in Concept 2: Metamorphosis and Anatomy. If children want to find and raise additional caterpillars, they will want to explore some of the resources and ideas suggested in Concept 3: Basic Needs and Concept 5: Variety. These experiences will help them learn how to provide for the needs of their particular species of butterfly through all the stages of its life cycle.

If your students are especially intrigued by the furriness of their caterpillar, you may want to guide them into some of the experiences suggested in Concept 4: Protective Behaviors. These experiences can help foster an understanding of how caterpillar hairs serve to discourage predators. You may also want to direct your students to some of the resources and experiences outlined in Concept 5: Variety. Children will learn through looking at pictures of different caterpillars that not all are furry, and they will become more aware of other differences that can be used to classify caterpillars into groups.

To locate and select learning experiences that will help children explore a particular question and discover an answer:

- Turn to the most closely related Concept in the Science section.

- Read the Background Information and skim through the Experiences section to find those experiences that respond directly to your students' question. You will find references to related learning activities described in the other sections of the Guide (Language Arts, Math, Music, etc.).

- After previewing all these activity suggestions, choose those experiences you feel will be most appropriate and meaningful for your students.

The "Sample Butterfly Inquiry: From Questions to Experiences" on the following page illustrates this planning process. This sample includes some of the questions raised by one group of students during their butterfly theme study, and shows how their teacher used the *Butterflies Abound* Guide to support their learning with appropriate learning experiences.

Adapting the Guide to Suit Younger and Older Students

Butterflies Abound can be used effectively with a variety of age groups. The children's questions and interests will determine which particular experiences are chosen for exploration. The activities are open-ended and can be explored by children at different levels of skill and sophistication. In general, younger students will need more teacher support, guidance, and demonstration. Older students, although requiring models and demonstration for new skills, will be able to work more independently.

In setting out to answer a question, older and younger students can both brainstorm possible avenues. Older students might go to the school library or use their classroom library to find the information and read the book independently or in small groups. The teacher of younger children might select a book and read it aloud to the class.

After listening to the book, younger children might respond orally, pictorially, or with their own approximated spelling. A written response might also take the form of shared writing, with the students contributing as much as they could with teacher guidance, and the teacher filling in the rest. Older children might take notes as they read, then decide how to organize and present the information that answers their original question. They might decide on a chart, a written report, a book, or an oral presentation accompanied with pictures.

We hope you experiment with many of the learning experiences and resources suggested in this Guide. If a particular experience suggests an excellent way to explore a question your students have posed, modify it to suit the needs of your class. Think of the skills and strategies your students have and those which they are ready to develop, and adapt the ideas accordingly.

SAMPLE BUTTERFLY INQUIRY: From Questions to Experiences

The purpose of this sample is to demonstrate how to move from the students' questions to experiences which offer them the opportunity to explore and answer those questions. You may wish to use a similar format as you select appropriate experiences in response to your own students' questions. All the Experiences listed here are included or cross-referenced in the indicated Science section.

Student Question: Do caterpillars of different butterflies look different?

Experiences:
Described in SCIENCE CONCEPT 5 - Variety and Classification
- Look at pictures in field guides.
- Chart the characteristics of different caterpillars seen in books.
- Read books about different butterflies.
- Draw, paint, and sculpt different caterpillars. (See ART.)
- Read the poem "Caterpillars." (See LANGUAGE ARTS.)
- Create a class Big Book: *We Like Caterpillars.* (See LANGUAGE ARTS: Writing Experiences.)
- Match pictures of different caterpillars to their adult butterfly form. (See MATH: Classifying.)

Student Question: How does a caterpillar become a butterfly?

Experiences:
Described in SCIENCE CONCEPT 2 - Metamorphosis and Anatomy. Section A: Overview.
- Observe the metamorphosis of the classroom butterfly.
- Record observations in journals, on reproducible Observation Sheets, on life cycle charts.
- Read books about the life cycle of different butterflies: *The Life of the Butterfly*, a Big Book by D. Drew about the Cabbage White butterfly; *Where Butterflies Grow* by J. Ryder, about Swallowtails; *Monarch Butterfly* by G. Gibbons.
- Make a life cycle mobile. (See ART.)
- Sing the songs "Metamorphosis" and "The Fuzzy Caterpillar." (See MUSIC.)
- Learn the finger play "Fuzzy Little Caterpillar" and the poems "Can You?" and "This Little Caterpillar." (See LANGUAGE ARTS.)
- Perform the Readers Theatre scripts, "What Will You Be?" and "I Wish I Could Fly." (See LANGUAGE ARTS.)
- Sequence the reproducible life cycle drawings. (See MATH.)
- Dramatize metamorphosis with stick puppets. (See DRAMATIC PLAY.)
- Create original metamorphosis songs, stories, and poems. (See LANGUAGE ARTS: Writing Experiences.)

Student Question: How many legs does a caterpillar have?

Experiences:
Described in SCIENCE CONCEPT 2 - Metamorphosis and Anatomy. Section C: The Caterpillar.
- Observe class caterpillar and count its legs.
- Examine and discuss the Butterflies Abound Poster, and diagrams and photos in books.
- Read *A First Look at Caterpillars* by Millicent Selsam and Joyce Hunt.
- Make anatomically correct caterpillars using clay, egg cartons, toothpicks, pipe cleaners, etc. (See ART.)

Student Question: What happens to butterflies in the winter?

Experiences:
Described in SCIENCE CONCEPT 3 - Basic Needs: Survival Behavior Related to Weather.
- Brainstorm and chart ideas of what other animals do in winter.
- Brainstorm and chart ideas of what butterflies might do in winter.
- Read about how butterflies overwinter: *Where Do They Go? Insects in Winter* by M. Selsam. Read pages 21–25.
- Research how different butterflies overwinter. Use the information to make a chart.
- Read the poem "About Caterpillars" by Aileen Fisher in *When It Comes to Bugs.*
- Sing "Winter Time." Create new verses. (See MUSIC.)
- Read about Monarch migration: *The Travels of Monarch X* by Ross Hutchins. Chart Monarch migration routes. (See SOCIAL STUDIES.)

Student Question: How does a butterfly eat?

Experiences:
Described in SCIENCE CONCEPT 2 - Metamorphosis and Anatomy, Section E: The Butterfly.
- Observe the classroom butterfly feeding.
- Examine the diagram of the butterfly's head on the Butterflies Abound Poster.
- Discuss the structure and use of the butterfly's proboscis. Look at close-up photos of the proboscis: *The Life of the Butterfly*, a Big Book by D. Drew, pages 14 and 16.
- Use a party blower as a model of the proboscis.
- Make Party Blower Butterflies. (See ART).
- Read the poem "Butterfly Tongues" by Aileen Fisher in *In the Woods, In the Meadow, In the Sky.*

SCIENCE

The life cycle of a butterfly is a fascinating occurrence. A tiny egg hatches and a caterpillar crawls out. The caterpillar eats and grows and changes into a seemingly lifeless chrysalis. Finally the chrysalis opens, a butterfly emerges, dries its wings, and flies away.

In order to experience the amazing transformation from caterpillar to butterfly and to explore the world of these insects, it is important that your students raise their own butterfly and observe the life cycle firsthand.

Appendix C provides a list of places offering mail-order caterpillars and chrysalises. Suggestions on how to find and care for the developing insect are offered within this Science section (Concept 3: Basic Needs and Behaviors).

The Science section is divided into five key concepts about butterflies. The concepts were developed from a review of important information and from the interest expressed by children. Each concept section begins with sample questions posed by students and teachers. **Background Information** provides teachers with a quick review of relevant scientific facts. The **Experiences** section suggests a wide variety of learning experiences that will help students explore and answer their questions. Related learning experiences offered in the other subject area sections (**Math, Music, Art,** etc.) are cross-referenced at the end of the Experiences section.

Concept 1: INSECTS
Butterflies belong to a group of animals called insects.

Students are encouraged to explore the characteristics common to all insects and view the butterfly within this larger, meaningful context.

Concept 2: METAMORPHOSIS and ANATOMY
During its lifetime, a butterfly passes through four stages. This process is called *metamorphosis*. The four stages are: *egg, caterpillar (larva), chrysalis (pupa), butterfly*. Each stage looks very different and has its own distinct anatomy.

This section provides the teacher with background information on the life cycle process and the distinctive features of each stage of the butterfly's development. The Experiences section suggests ideas for studying your classroom egg, caterpillar, chrysalis, and butterfly.

Concept 3: BASIC NEEDS and BEHAVIORS
Each stage of a butterfly (egg, caterpillar, chrysalis, and butterfly) needs certain conditions in order to develop. Each stage has survival behaviors and adaptations that help it meet the challenges of its environment.

This section includes information and experiences related to raising butterflies in the classroom and understanding how butterflies survive outdoors. Feeding behaviors, reproductive behaviors, and survival behaviors related to weather and seasonal changes are explored. If you are raising Monarch butterflies in the fall, the migration information and experiences will be of particular interest.

Concept 4: PROTECTIVE BEHAVIORS
Each stage of a butterfly (egg, caterpillar, chrysalis, and butterfly) has behaviors and adaptations that help it escape predators.

Camouflage, evasive flight patterns, and mimicry are among the defensive behaviors examined in this section.

Concept 5: VARIETY/CLASSIFICATION
The eggs, caterpillars, chrysalises, and butterflies of different species display a wide range of shapes, colors, and sizes. Scientists classify butterflies into families according to certain shared attributes.

Children compare different butterfly species in all stages of development, then classify them according to various criteria of their choosing. The scientific classification of butterflies is examined, and children are encouraged to research and compare specific butterfly species.

These five science concepts do not have to be explored in any particular order. Certain concepts may be of particular interest to certain students. Often several concepts will be explored simultaneously. For example, when the classroom insect is a caterpillar, students will want to learn about the anatomy of a caterpillar and the general concept of metamorphosis (Concept 2). They may also want to know about the conditions caterpillars need in order to grow and thrive (Concept 3). Some students may wonder why a caterpillar is considered an insect but a worm is not (Concept 1). The Introduction offers other suggestions for using students' questions and interests to direct the focus of your butterfly theme study.

The experiences suggested in the Science section are designed to expand the children's knowledge of butterflies and to provide opportunities for them to use the following science process skills:

brainstorming	recognizing patterns, sequences	predicting
asking questions	drawing from observations	inferring
observing	recording information	forming hypothesis
comparing	organizing information	drawing conclusions
classifying, sorting	constructing and interpreting graphs	using scientific equipment

What kind of animal is a butterfly?

What kind of animal is a caterpillar?

How can you tell if an animal is an insect?

Are moths and butterflies the same thing?

Do all insects start off as one thing and become another like the butterfly?

How long have butterflies and other insects lived on the earth?

Concept 1: INSECTS

Butterflies belong to a group of animals called insects.

Background Information

Butterflies and moths belong to a group of animals we call insects. Insects are the most plentiful animals in the world. Fossil evidence shows that insects have existed on the earth for 300–400 million years. The oldest butterfly fossil is about 40 million years old. Moths appeared 100–140 years ago.

The adult insect is an animal with six jointed legs, two antennae, two eyes, and two or four wings if wings are present. It has three main body parts: the head, thorax, and abdomen. Insects do not have bones or an internal skeleton. They have an exoskeleton, a hard skin or shell on the outside of their bodies.

The class of animals called insects (*Insecta*) is divided into about thirty orders. Butterflies and moths belong to an order called *Lepidoptera. Lepidoptera* means "scale-winged." Butterflies and moths are distinct from other insects because they have scales over all or most of their wings and often their body as well. Moths and butterflies are similar, but they differ in several ways. The chart below lists basic differences between most moths and most butterflies. Note that there are exceptions to every difference listed.

Moths	Butterflies
• most are nocturnal (active during the night)	• most are diurnal (active during the day)
• most hold wings horizontally when at rest	• most hold wings vertically when at rest
• most have feathered or thread-like antennae	• most have clubbed antennae
• most spin a cocoon	• most form a chrysalis
• most have thick bodies	• most have long, thin bodies

Not all insects go through a complete metamorphosis like a butterfly. Different types of development in insects include:

- **No Metamorphosis** The adult looks the same as the young with the only difference being size, i.e. silverfish, spring tail.
- **Simple, Direct, or Incomplete Metamorphosis** The adult may be, but not always, very similar to its young. The adult may have wings and the young may not, i.e. grasshopper, dragonfly, cicada, cricket, termite, praying mantis.
- **Complete, Indirect Metamorphosis** There are sharply defined stages which look very different from the adult, i.e. moth, butterfly, beetle, wasps, bees, ant, firefly, housefly.

Experiences

- Ask the children to name all the insects they can. As the responses are given write them down on large chart paper for all to see.

Insects
cricket
grasshopper
mosquito
ant
fly

- Review the list to see if anyone disagrees with any of the choices. Ask questions such as: *Why don't you think it is an insect? Why do you think it is an insect?* If the children have not mentioned them ask, *Are butterflies and moths insects?*

- With your students, gather books about insects and collect insect pictures. Together, create a classroom resource center and display. Share some of the following books. (See the Bibliography for more information.)

  Backyard Insects by Millicent E. Selsam
  Bugs by Nancy Winslow Parker and Joan Richards Wright
  A First Look at Insects by Millicent E. Selsam
  The Icky Bug Alphabet Book by Jerry Pallotta
  An Insect's Body by Joanna Cole
  Insects by Illa Podendorf

- Many of the books just listed have clear, close-up photos or drawings of common insects. Display pictures of several insects and ask, *What do you think is the same about all insects?* List the shared characteristics that the children suggest on a chart. You may wish to correct and/or add information.

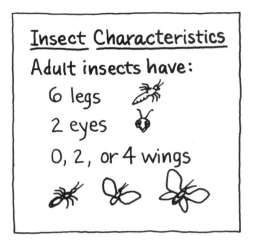

- Provide a collection of animal pictures or toy animals. Encourage children to sort them into two categories: **insect** and **noninsect**. Have the children verify their answers by checking to see which animals have the characteristics they listed on their Insect Characteristics chart: 6 legs, 3 body parts, etc.

- Collect living and dead insects for observation and display. Be cautious when gathering and handling insects because some sting or bite. The children can use resource books to help them identify and label the insects.

- In order to keep the dead insects from being damaged, but available for viewing, place them in a box on a layer of cotton or glue them to the bottom of a box. Cover the box with plastic wrap. Another way to display the insects is to push a long pin through the body and then stick the pin in a piece of wood, clay, or styrofoam. Label the collection.

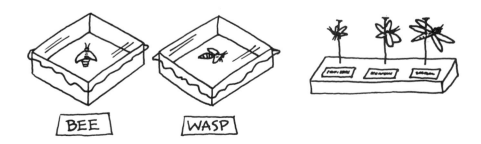

- Live "bugs" can be collected and kept for a short period of time in an "insect zoo." Research to find the best ways to care for these live animals. Many are hard to care for and are best released at the end of the school day. Have a child be the entomologist of the day and give guided tours of the "insect museum" and/or "insect zoo."

```
┌─────────────┐  ┌─────────────┐
│ Insects that│  │ Insects in  │
│ have visited│  │ our Museum  │
│ for a day   │  │ butterfly   │
│ cricket     │  │ moth        │
│ housefly    │  │ bee         │
│             │  │ cicada      │
└─────────────┘  └─────────────┘
```

- Keep hand lenses near the insect collection(s) for viewing purposes. Encourage children to count the legs, compare the colors, shapes, body parts, etc.

- Compare the gathered "bugs" to the list of Insect Characteristics. Are they all insects? If not, sort into two groups: insects and not insects. Children may also enjoy sorting by other characteristics: color, size, bite people/don't bite people, etc.

- If there is a moth and a butterfly in your collection, compare and discuss observed differences. Photographs of a moth and a butterfly can also be compared. Chart the children's comments. You may want to share the "Moth or Butterfly?" picture chart on the back cover of the Big Book, *Caterpillar Diary* by David Drew (see Bibliography). Some teachers raise both a moth and a butterfly in their classroom for comparison purposes.

- For more information on the following topics, read some of the books listed below. See the Bibliography for additional information:

General Information
Familiar Insects and Spiders. An Audubon Society Pocket Guide
Let's Look at Insects by Harriet Huntington

Differences Between Moths and Butterflies
Amazing World of Butterflies and Moths by Louis Sabin
Amazing Butterflies & Moths by John Still

Insect Metamorphosis
Insect Metamorphosis by Ron and Nancy Goor

Activities to Do with Insects
Bug Wise by Pamela Hickman
Insect Almanac by Monica Russo

- Provide an assortment of scraps and art materials. Have children draw or construct an imaginary insect. Display the Insect Characteristics chart near the art area. Children may enjoy naming their new insect species and writing a description: where it lives, what it eats, interesting habits.

- Read the picture book *I Wish I Were a Butterfly* written by James Howe and illustrated by Ed Young. Which of the characters in the book are insects? Have students describe the characteristics of individual insects. Ask students which insects they think are most attractive. See the **Language Arts** section for additional suggestions for extending children's involvement with this story.

- Read poems about insects. Information for locating the following poems is provided in the Poetry section of the Bibliography.

   "Every Insect" by Dorothy Aldis in *Eric Carle's Animals Animals*
   "The Insects' World" by Ethel Jacobson in *Poetry Place Anthology*

- Take a field trip to entomology/zoology department of a museum or university.

- Invite a guest speaker (amateur or professional entomologist or lepidopterist) to talk about insects and/or show an insect collection.

NOTES

Does a butterfly egg get bigger and bigger before it hatches?

Which end is the caterpillar's head?

What's that white stuff the caterpillar is making?

What is happening inside the chrysalis?

How does the butterfly get out of the chrysalis?

Concept 2: METAMORPHOSIS and ANATOMY

During its lifetime, a butterfly passes through four stages. This process is called metamorphosis. The four stages are: egg, caterpillar (larva), chrysalis (pupa), butterfly. Each stage looks very different and has its own distinct anatomy.

Butterfly Metamorphosis and Anatomy is a major focus of any butterfly theme study. For convenience, we have divided Concept 2 into five sections. Background Information and Learning Experiences are offered in each section.

  A. Butterfly Metamorphosis: An Overview

  B. The Egg

  C. The Caterpillar (or Larva)

  D. The Chrysalis (or Pupa)

  E. The Butterfly

A. BUTTERFLY METAMORPHOSIS: AN OVERVIEW

Background Information

To become an adult, a butterfly goes through four stages that are collectively called *metamorphosis,* a Greek word meaning "change in form."

The difference between the four stages of metamorphosis are so great that without previous experience it would be difficult for anyone to assume a relationship between them. For young children it is important that they experience the entire growth cycle in sequence in order to understand the connection between the various stages.

Although every butterfly goes through the same stages in the same order, there are variations from one butterfly species to another within each stage.

Experiences

- Visit the butterfly center often to observe the developing insect. Use hand lenses to examine details. Encourage child-initiated visits to the center. Some of the most meaningful learning takes place during these unscheduled observation times.

- Record questions, observations, data, and drawings on class charts and webs, and in individual journals and learning logs. The reproducible Observation Sheet provided in Appendix A may be useful. See the **Language Arts** section (Writing Experiences) for suggestions.

- Create and illustrate poems, songs, stories, and plays inspired by the butterfly metamorphosis experience. See the **Language Arts** section for suggestions (Writing Experiences: Poetry, Books).

- Make a graph of the butterfly life cycle. See the **Math** section (Graphing).

- Make and label observational drawings of each stage. Use these drawings to make life cycle charts, mobiles, spinners, or puzzles suggested in the **Art** section (Life Cycle).

- Sequence the different stages of the butterfly life cycle using puzzles, photographs, puppets, or the reproducible life cycle pictures in Appendix A. See the **Math** section (Sequencing) for more ideas.

- Make a board game that takes a butterfly through its life cycle and its encounters with nature and people. See the **Math** section (Counting/Estimating) for suggestions.

- Dramatize the life cycle of a butterfly with hand or finger puppets, with felt characters on the flannel board, or with children acting out various stages. See the **Art** section (Life Cycle) for puppet and costume suggestions and the **Dramatic Play** section for additional ideas (Felt Board, Puppet Theater, Butterfly Performances).

- Set up a Metamorphosis Obstacle Course on the playground. See the **Physical Activities** section for specific suggestions.

- Read nonfiction books with the metamorphosis theme:

  * *Caterpillar Diary* by David Drew (Big Book)
  * *The Life of the Butterfly* by David Drew (Big Book)
  * *Sometimes Things Change* by Patricia Eastman (Big Book)
  * *Life of the Butterfly* by Heiderose and Andreas Fischer-Nagel
  * *Monarch Butterfly* by Gail Gibbons

* *Where Butterflies Grow* by Joanne Ryder
Butterflies by Althea Braithwaite
Butterfly by Michael Chinery
The Butterfly by Paula Z. Hogan
Animals and Their Young by Lada Josefa Kratky (Big Book)
Butterflies Becoming by Bill Martin, Jr.
From Egg to Butterfly by Marlene Reidel

- Read fiction books with the metamorphosis theme:

* *The Very Hungry Caterpillar* by Eric Carle
* *The Caterpillar and the Polliwog* by Jack Kent
A Caterpillar's Wish, by the First Graders of A.R. Shepherd School
A New Friend for Morganfield by Ann Hobart
Sally's Caterpillar by Anne and Harlow Rockwell
Terry and the Caterpillar by Millicent Selsam

See the **Bibliography** and the **Language Arts** section (Reading Experiences) for more information. An asterisk (*) before a book title means that specific Experiences suggestions for that book are offered in the **Language Arts** section (Reading Experiences).

- Look at photographs in reference books. Use the illustrations in the Big Books *Caterpillar Diary* and *The Life of the Butterfly* by David Drew or the companion wall charts to discuss the anatomy of the different stages of the life cycle.

- Look at the Painted Lady Life Cycle Poster. See the Bibliography for ordering information.

- Enjoy some of the following finger plays, poems, and chants. The words are provided in the **Language Arts** section. Additional pieces are recommended for each life stage of the butterfly. (See the other four subsections of Science: Concept 2.)

  Finger plays: "The Caterpillar," "Fuzzy Wuzzy Caterpillar," "One Little Egg," "A Chrysalis," "Fuzzy Little Caterpillar"

  Poems: "Caterpillar" by Christina Rossetti, "Can You?", "This Little Caterpillar," "The Butterfly"

  Chants: "What Do You Get?," "Birth of a Butterfly"

- Perform the Readers Theatre scripts: "What Will You Be?", "I Wish I Could Fly." See the **Language Arts** section.

- Sing the following songs, set to familiar tunes: "I'm a Little Caterpillar," "Metamorphosis," "Where?", "The Fuzzy Caterpillar." The words are provided in the **Music** section.

- Learn the songs "Caterpillars on the Run" by Stephen Titra and "The Caterpillar" by Emilie Poulssen. For more information, see the **Music** section of the Bibliography.

- Read some of the poems listed in the Bibliography. The following poems are particularly appropriate for the topic of metamorphosis:

  "Butterfly Wings" by Aileen Fisher in *In the Woods, In the Meadow, In the Sky*

  "Twice Born" by Aileen Fisher in *Out in the Dark and Daylight*

  "Cocoons" by Aileen Fisher in *Inside a Little House*

  "Caterpillar, Caterpillar" by Helen J. Fletcher in *Finger Play Poems and Stories*

  "The Butterfly and the Caterpillar" by Joseph Lauren in *Rainbow in the Sky*

  "Cocoon" by David McCord in *All Small*

  "Fuzzy Wuzzy, Creepy Crawly" by Lillian Schulz in *Read-Aloud Rhymes for the Very Young*

  "Caterpillar's Lullaby" by Jane Yolen in *Dragon Night*

NOTES

B. THE EGG

Background Information

The female butterfly locates and then lays eggs on the particular plant that will be needed for food by the young caterpillar. The eggs are laid either singly, in rows, in chains, or in masses of a few to several hundred eggs. Sometimes the female butterfly lets the eggs scatter as she flies above the caterpillar host plant. A special "glue" produced by the female butterfly is used to attach the eggs to surfaces such as leaves, stems, and bark.

The eggs of the butterfly are covered by a strong membrane which, although not brittle, can be compared to an eggshell. Each egg contains the germ of a future caterpillar and the liquid food necessary for its growth. Butterfly eggs vary from species to species. They assume many shapes—conical, domed, turban-shaped, pin cushion-shaped and spindle-shaped. The surface texture can be ridged, pitted, smooth, or can contain raised projections.

Butterfly eggs

Newly laid eggs are usually yellowish-white and soft. As they harden, the colors may change substantially. Eggs can be white, green, yellow, brown, blue, or red. Some have dots and lines of darker colors. Sometimes the egg membrane is transparent and the developing caterpillar within can be seen.

All butterfly eggs are tiny: about the size of the head on a straight pin. The largest butterfly egg is about 1/8 inches across.

The time it takes for an egg to develop varies from a few days or weeks to nine months if the butterfly overwinters as an egg. In many instances the caterpillar's first meal is the "eggshell." Many caterpillars will not develop properly unless they have ingested the shell—it contains nutrients necessary for the insect's growth.

Experiences

- Initial Observation: If butterfly eggs are available, gather the children in small groups to view the egg(s). Provide hand lenses. Encourage observation, discussion, and speculation. Record questions and comments on an Egg Observation class chart. This observation chart and those for the other stages can be written on large chart paper and displayed in the classroom when completed.

Note: Since butterfly eggs are so small, they are difficult to find and identify. If eggs are not available, pictures in reference books will help children develop an understanding of the features and size of a butterfly egg.

Pose questions to guide and extend the children's observations: *What color is the egg? How would you describe its shape? Is the texture smooth? Can you think of an object that is the same size?*

- Look at and discuss close-up photographs and drawings of butterfly eggs in books. Be sure students understand that the pictures are greatly enlarged. Clarify the actual size of an egg. This is particularly important if children do not have access to real butterfly eggs. The following books include particularly good photographs of various kinds of butterfly eggs: *Butterfly & Moth* by Paul Whalley and *Butterfly and Caterpillar* by Barrie Watts.

- Begin a science journal or learning log. Record questions, observations, thoughts, data, and drawings. The reproducible Observation Sheets provided in Appendix A may be useful. See the **Language Arts** section (Writing Experiences: Journals, Learning Logs, and Observation Sheets) for more detail.

- Later Observations: If you have real butterfly eggs, look again to see if the color has changed. Add the children's comments and questions to the Egg Observation class chart. Again, you may wish to pose questions to extend thinking: *Do you think the size of the egg changed? Do you think that the texture has changed? Has the color changed? Can you see inside the egg?*

- Begin a life cycle graph. See the **Math** section (Graphing) for suggestions.

- Make and label observational drawings of the egg for a life cycle chart, puzzle, spinner, or mobile. See the **Art** section (Life Cycle) for details.

- Enjoy the following fingerplay and chant. The words are provided in the **Language Arts** section.

  Finger play: "One Little Egg"

  Chant: "What Do You Get?"

- Help students create a Readers Theatre script based on Eric Carle's book *The Very Busy Spider.* The Readers Theatre script can be entitled, "The Very Busy Butterfly." Suggest that the butterfly be very busy laying eggs. See the **Language Arts** section (Readers Theatre) for suggestion on developing and performing the script.

NOTES

C. THE CATERPILLAR (OR LARVA)

Background Information

All caterpillars are structurally alike. They differ in size, color, and shape. In general, a caterpillar is a wormlike creature with a hard round head. Its body is divided into three parts: the *head,* the *thorax,* and the *abdomen.* Together, the thorax and abdomen contain twelve to fourteen segments. Joints between the segments allow the caterpillar to bend and move its body in any direction.

Caterpillar Anatomy

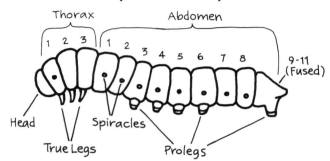

The caterpillar's thorax consists of three segments. Each segment has a pair of true legs. Each leg ends in a sharp claw.

The caterpillar's abdomen consists of nine to eleven segments. The final two (or three) abdominal segments are fused. The third, fourth, fifth, sixth segments and the last fused segment of the abdomen contain pairs of *prolegs.* Although not true legs in terms of structure, they function as legs. Groups of tiny hooks called *crochets* on the tip of each proleg help the caterpillar cling to objects. Other insects with prolegs do not have crochets. The prolegs on the last segment are called *anal claspers.*

Breathing holes, called *spiracles,* are found in pairs. There is a spiracle on each side of every segment except the second and third thoracic segments and the last abdominal segment.

The caterpillar's head is conspicuous and varies in form and size. It contains two short *antennae,* ten to twelve tiny eyes known as *ocelli,* and mouth parts. Even with five or six ocelli on each side of its head, the caterpillar's vision is poor.

Caterpillar Head

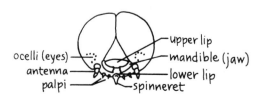

The caterpillar's primary purpose is to eat and grow. It is equipped with very strong jaws. Between the upper and lower lips are two spoon-shaped *mandibles* which contain numerous teeth. The *spinneret,* the duct opening of the silk gland, is located on the lower lip. Also located on the lips are two organs called the *palpi.* Both the palpi and the antennae are useful in guiding the weak-eyed caterpillar.

The *cuticle* or "skin" that covers the caterpillar is made of *chitin.* The cuticle is the insect's exoskeleton. The cuticle can be smooth, or hairy, or have horny projections or spines. Although caterpillar coloration is extremely varied, most caterpillars are shades of green or brown. Some caterpillars, however, are brightly colored.

The cuticle can stretch only a limited amount. As it grows, the caterpillar must *molt,* or shed its skin. Before molting, the caterpillar grows a new skin beneath the old. When the cuticle gets tight, a gland releases a slippery fluid between the old and the new skin. This fluid aids the molting process.

When the caterpillar molts, the cuticle on the back of the head splits first. The split continues down the back of the caterpillar and the old skin becomes loose. The caterpillar pulls itself out of the old skin. The new skin is temporarily soft to allow for a spurt of growth. The caterpillar takes in air and stretches its cuticle. Then the new enlarged skin hardens.

If you wish to observe and record the dates of your caterpillar's molts, you will have to observe the caterpillar closely. When a caterpillar stops eating, it is usually preparing to molt. Reference books may provide information regarding the number of molts and the length of time your species is a caterpillar.

The molted cuticle, called the *exuvia,* will be a little disk of rumpled skin. If your caterpillar cage is clean, it will be easier to find the exuvia. Sometimes the colors of the caterpillar and other features such as the head, the spine, or prominences can be seen.

The period between molts is called an *instar.* A caterpillar generally goes through four to six instars. During the final instar, when the caterpillar is ready to pupate, it stops eating and spins a silk pad on a secure surface with its spinneret. Then the caterpillar entangles its anal claspers in the silk pad.

The hanging position of caterpillars varies. Some species form their chrysalis while the caterpillar is hanging upside down. Other species pupate with the caterpillar upright. In this case the caterpillar spins a silk line, called a *girdle,* to hold itself upright.

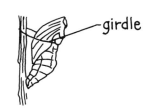

Cremaster   girdle

Beneath the skin of the caterpillar, the outer layer of the chrysalis is forming. As the caterpillar twists and wiggles, its skin splits and shrivels from the head to the abdomen. As this is happening the pupating caterpillar stabs a newly formed stem, called a *cremaster,* into the silk pad, replacing the anal claspers. The cremaster has a series of microscopic hooks on the end which form a very secure attachment to the silk pad. If the students observe the caterpillar pupating, have them watch carefully for this step. They may be able to see the cremaster appear and become attached to the silk pad.

A chrysalis that hangs upside down must free the end of its body from the molting skin and attach its cremaster directly to the silk pad. To avoid falling during this maneuver, it holds on to the old skin with two projections beneath the cremaster. Chrysalises that are upright are supported by their silk girdle during this process.

Experiences

- Initial Observation: Gather the children in small groups to look at the caterpillar. Make hand lenses available. Encourage discussion and speculation. Record the children's questions and comments on a Caterpillar Observation class chart.

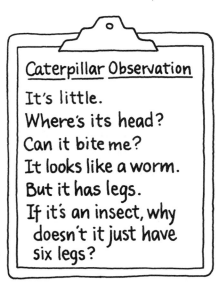

Caterpillar Observation

It's little.
Where's its head?
Can it bite me?
It looks like a worm.
But it has legs.
If it's an insect, why
 doesn't it just have
 six legs?

Note: When you observe the caterpillar, leave it on its food source so it does not get injured through handling. The children can watch the caterpillar eating the leaf.

You may wish to pose questions to guide the children's observations and discussion: *Where's the caterpillar's head? How can you tell? What do you see on its head? Do you think a caterpillar can see and smell? Do you think it has teeth? How many legs can you see? Do they all look alike? How does the caterpillar move? In what directions can it bend?*

- Encourage children to visit the caterpillar cage often on their own, to discuss their observations with their classmates, and to record their thoughts and questions in writing and drawings.

- Before formally looking at the caterpillar again, review the comments and questions from the first group observation and children's independent observations. Then display the Butterflies Abound Poster.

  Help children relate their real-life caterpillar observations to the labeled caterpillar diagram. Discuss parts of the caterpillar they might not have seen in order to expand their knowledge. The parts of the head, the segments, the three sections of the body, and the spiracles are difficult and sometimes impossible to see on a live caterpillar, especially if it is hairy.

  Look at the classroom caterpillar again so the students can view, discuss, and validate the new information and develop new questions. Add comments and questions to the Caterpillar Observation class chart.

- Begin or continue individual science journals or learning logs. Have students record questions, observations, data, and drawings. You may wish to use one of the reproducible Observation Sheets provided in Appendix A. See the **Language Arts** section (Writing Experiences: Journals and Learning Logs) for more detail.

- Later observations: Ask the children if they notice any changes in the caterpillar. *Is it the same size? Has the color or pattern changed? Does the head look different? Do you think it has molted? Why?* Record the children's comments and questions on the Caterpillar Observation class chart.

- Begin or continue to record data on a life cycle graph. If possible, record the dates on which your caterpillar molts and pupates. See the **Math** section (Graphing) for suggestions.

- Measure the length of the caterpillar. Chart its growth every few days. See the **Math** section (Graphing) for details.

- Make and label observational drawings of the caterpillar for a life cycle chart, puzzle, spinner, or mobile. See the **Art** section (Life Cycle) for details.

- Review caterpillar body parts as you sing "See the Caterpillar Train" to the tune of "Dem Bones." As they sing, children can act out the words, forming a Caterpillar Train. See the **Music** and **Physical Activities** sections for details.

- Enjoy the following finger plays, poems, and chant. Words are provided in the **Language Arts** section.

  Finger plays: "Fuzzy Wuzzy Caterpillar," "Fuzzy Little Caterpillar"

  Poems: "I Can Spell," "This Little Caterpillar," "Little Ms. Muffet," "Five Little Caterpillars"

Chant: "Arabella Miller Chant"

- Sing the song "Little Arabella Miller" to the tune of "Twinkle, Twinkle Little Star." The words and accompanying motions are provided in the **Music** section.

- Read some of the poems about caterpillars listed in the Bibliography.

  "Caterpillars" by Aileen Fisher in *Cricket in the Thicket* or *Surprises*
  "Ten Little Caterpillars" by Bill Martin, Jr. in *Bill Martin Jr.'s Treasury Chest*
  "Patter Pitter Caterpillar" by Jack Prelutsky in *Beneath a Blue Umbrella*
  "The Tickle Rhyme" by Ian Serraillier in *The Random House Book of Poetry for Children*
  "Only My Opinion" by Monica Shannon in *Read-Aloud Rhymes for the Very Young* and in *Eric Carle's Animals Animals*

- Encourage children to create original poems, songs, and books inspired by their caterpillar observations and experiences. See the **Language Arts** section for suggestions (Writing Experiences: Poetry, Books).

- Look at photographs of caterpillars. Many of the nonfiction books listed below contain excellent pictures. Additional photos can be found in reference books (see Bibliography).

- Make caterpillar pictures and sculptures from a variety of materials. Encourage children to include as many anatomical details as possible. Display the Butterflies Abound Poster as reference. Some useful materials include clay, egg carton sections, round objects, and round pieces of paper. See the **Art** section (Caterpillars) for additional ideas.

- Explore patterns found on caterpillars. Refer to the **Math** section (Sequencing) and the **Art** section (Caterpillars) for ideas.

- Act out caterpillar behaviors and movements. See **Dramatic Play** (Movement) for suggestions.

- Do cooking projects with a caterpillar theme. See the **Cooking** section.

- Read nonfiction books about caterpillars.

  * *Caterpillar Diary* by David Drew (Big Book)
    A First Look at Caterpillars by Millicent E. Selsam.
    Caterpillars by Dorothy Sterling
    Caterpillars and *Butterfly and Caterpillar* by Barrie Watts
    Butterfly & Moth by Paul Whalley

- Read fiction books with a caterpillar theme.

  * *The Very Hungry Caterpillar* by Eric Carle (Big Book available)
  * *Charlie the Caterpillar* by Dom DeLuise
  * *The Longest Journey in the World* by William Barrett Morris (Big Book)
    The Caterpillar Story by Achim Broger
    I Like Caterpillars by Gladys Conklin
    The Caterpillar and the Butterfly by Ruth Lieberherr-Kubler
    Down the River Without a Paddle by Robert and Claire Wiest

See the Bibliography and the **Language Arts** section (Reading Experiences) for more information. An asterisk (*) before a book title means that specific Experiences suggestions for that book are offered in the **Language Arts** section (Reading Experiences).

- Create a Readers Theatre script for *The Very Hungry Caterpillar* by Eric Carle. See the **Language Arts** section (Readers Theatre) for more details.

NOTES

D. THE CHRYSALIS (OR PUPA)

Background Information

Chrysalises come in a variety of shapes, textures, and colors. Some are green or brown and resemble leaves, twigs, or pieces of wood. Others have bright variegated colors. Some are covered with small bumps.

Chrysalises

Most are attached to a leaf, twig, or other surface by the cremaster. (See Caterpillar Background Information for more details.) Some types of chrysalises are suspended upside down, other types hang diagonally head up. In the latter case, a silk line called a girdle is wrapped around the main part of the chrysalis and holds it securely in position.

A chrysalis is different from a cocoon. A cocoon is a covering spun by a moth caterpillar. The caterpillar pupates inside the cocoon. The chrysalis covering is formed beneath the caterpillar's skin and appears as it molts for the final time.

The covering of the chrysalis is made of chitin. This is the same material that forms the cuticle or skin of the caterpillar. There are spiracles, or breathing holes, in the chrysalis' chitin for the purpose of respiration.

When first formed, the chrysalis may wiggle. Then the skin will harden and the chrysalis will hang, seemingly inert. However, inside the chrysalis a transformation is taking place: one animal is dissolving and another is being constructed.

Inside the chrysalis, the tissues of the caterpillar dissolve into a "liquid." The cells that make up this liquid begin to reassemble and form a new body—a butterfly. Soon after the formation of a chrysalis the outlines of certain butterfly features can be seen on the surface. These lines appear before the full development of the structures of the butterfly.

The time from the formation of the chrysalis to the emergence of the butterfly varies from about ten days to six months or more, depending on the species, the weather, and if the butterfly overwinters as a chrysalis. The outer covering of some chrysalises becomes transparent prior to hatching and the colors of the developing butterfly can be seen within. Butterflies usually emerge from their chrysalises on warm, sunny mornings.

Experiences

- Initial Observation: Gather the children in small groups to view the chrysalis. Record their comments and questions on a Chrysalis Observation class chart.

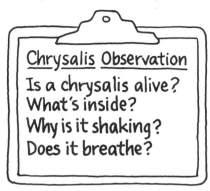

Chrysalis Observation
Is a chrysalis alive?
What's inside?
Why is it shaking?
Does it breathe?

Pose questions to extend observations and guide the discussion: *What color is the chrysalis? Is it shiny? dull? smooth? rough? How is it attached?*

- Later observations: Have children observe and record any changes on the Chrysalis Observation class chart. Pose questions: *Is the chrysalis the same shape, texture, size, color? Has it changed places or moved?*

- Begin or continue to update science journals or learning logs. Students should add new chrysalis questions, thoughts, observations, data, and drawings. You may wish to use one of the reproducible Observation Sheets provided in Appendix A. See the **Language Arts** section (Writing Experiences: Journals, Learning Logs, and Observation Sheets) for more details.

- Make and label observational drawings of the chrysalis for a life cycle chart, puzzle, spinner, or mobile. See the **Art** section (Life Cycle) for details.

- Continue to record data on a life cycle graph. See **Math** section (Graphing) for information.

- If you have watched several classroom caterpillars pupate, number the chrysalises in the order in which they formed. Speculate and observe whether butterflies emerge from the chrysalises in the same order.

- Look in reference books to find pictures of different chrysalises and create an awareness of the range of shapes, textures, colors, and positions. Photographs of a wide variety of chrysalises are included in *Butterfly & Moth* by Paul Whalley.

- Discuss the differences between a chrysalis and a cocoon. (See Background Information.) In poetry and fiction, authors often refer to a chrysalis as a "cocoon." Have children examine books and poems to find examples of this "mistake." Discuss why the authors and poets might have made this error. Did they not know the difference? Did they decide to use the wrong word for a reason? (Maybe it's just too hard to find a word that rhymes with chrysalis!)

- Enjoy the following finger plays. The words are provided in the **Language Arts** section.

  "The Caterpillar," "Fuzzy Little Caterpillar," "A Chrysalis"

- Practice and perform "Chrysalis Diary," a poem for two voices by Paul Fleischman. See the Bibliography for more information.

- Share some other chrysalis and cocoon poems. See the Bibliography for further information.

  "Cocoons" by Aileen Fisher in *Inside a Little House*

  "Cocoon" by David McCord in *All Small*

  "Caterpillar's Lullaby" by Jane Yolen in *Dragon Night*

  "Message from a Caterpillar" by Lilian Moore in *Something New Begins*

- Encourage children to create original poems, songs, and books inspired by their chrysalis observations and experiences. See the **Language Arts** section for suggestions (Writing Experiences: Poetry, Books).

NOTES

E. THE BUTTERFLY

Background Information

The butterfly splits the skin of the chrysalis casing and crawls out. Its legs grasp the skin of the chrysalis, and then any available perch. It hangs with a huge abdomen and small crumpled wings. As the butterfly pumps blood into its wings, the wings enlarge and flatten and the butterfly's body becomes smaller. There is a discharge of red or yellow liquid called *meconium*. Approximately an hour after emerging, the wings assume their full shape and become dry.

The butterfly's tongue, called a *proboscis,* is a long thin tube that works like a drinking straw. When it's not in use, it is kept coiled up. The two sides of the proboscis develop separately in the chrysalis stage. After the butterfly emerges from the chrysalis, it uncoils and coils the two halves of the proboscis. In doing so, it "zips" together the series of hooks and spines along the edges of the two sections, forming a tube for drinking.

Many butterflies have a short life span of about two weeks, but some live six to eight months. In order to reproduce, most butterflies need to quickly mate and lay eggs.

The male usually searches for the female. He recognizes her by color, pattern, and odor. The male will only mate with the female if she sends the correct signal. Butterflies mate by joining at the tip of their abdomen when facing in opposite directions. The male squeezes the end of the female's abdomen with his anal claspers. The sperm enters the female's abdomen and is stored there. Later when each egg comes out of the abdomen it is fertilized by the stored sperm. The female butterfly either lays these eggs singly, in rows, or in masses on the particular plant that will be needed as food for the young caterpillars, or she lets the eggs scatter as she flies above the plant.

The butterfly has four wings and three main body parts: the *head,* the *thorax,* and the *abdomen*.

Butterfly Anatomy

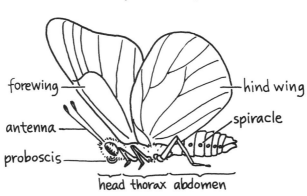

The butterfly's head is rounded and has a pair of large compound eyes, each made up of thousands of tiny hexagonal lenses that look something like the sections of a honeycomb. Though the eyes do not move, the butterfly can see in all directions due to the many different angles at which its lenses are aimed. Butterflies can see shapes, motion, and both visible and ultraviolet light.

Below the eyes are two hairy projections called the *palpi*. Between the palpi is the *proboscis,* the butterfly's mouth. The butterfly uses its proboscis like a drinking straw, sucking nectar from plants, juice from fruit or sap trees, or moisture from dung or carrion. When the proboscis is not in use it is rolled up. The butterfly is the only insect that has a curling proboscis.

Butterfly Head

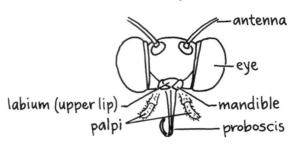

The butterfly's *antennae* are found between the eyes. Some scientists believe the primary function of the antennae is to "taste" the air and act somewhat like a combination of our nose and tongue. Others believe the primary function is balance and orientation. Each antenna consists of short segments. Some antennae clubs are rounded; others are thin or hooked at the end.

The *thorax* is the "engine" part of the butterfly's body. It contains strong muscles which move the legs and wings. The thorax is divided into three sections. Because the body is covered with hair these divisions are not easy to see. The placement of the legs and wings on the three parts is as follows:

the *prothorax* - first pair of legs

the *mesathorax* - second pair of legs and front pair of wings

the *metathorax* - third pair of legs and hind pair of wings

Some butterflies have a *tympana* on the thorax, a body part that picks up sound vibrations.

The butterfly has four wings, two on each side of its body. Butterfly wing shapes vary. They can be nearly round, triangular, squarish, clipped, long, or hooked. A butterfly's opposing wings are symmetrical in pattern, shape, and vein arrangement. Generally, the forewings are larger than the hind wings and overlap them. Each hind wing has a projection called the *humeral lobe* that underlaps the forewing and holds the wings together. Sometimes male and female butterflies of the same species have differences in their wing colors and patterns.

The structure of a butterfly wing can be compared to a sandwich. The bread is the clear and very thin sheet of chitin. The filling contains air spaces and veins. As the newly emerged butterfly's wings dry, the two layers of chitin merge except along the veins.

Scales of many different shapes and sizes are attached to both sides of the butterfly's wing. These scales overlap, like shingles on a roof. They are very small. There can be as many as 100 in a row one inch long. The scales give the wings their color. They produce colors in two different ways. Some scales contain chemicals or pigments that produce the colors red, orange, yellow, brown, black, and white. Others have surfaces that act like prisms to bend and scatter light. These scales produce blues, silvers, violets, and greens. One butterfly can have both kinds of color scales. Sex scales called *androconia* are also found on some butterflies' wings. These scales produce scent hormones or pheromones to attract mates.

Butterfly Scales

All butterflies have three pairs of legs. In one family of butterflies known as "brush footed" or "four footed," the tiny forelegs are hard to see. Each pair of legs is slightly different, but all are similar in structure. Each leg is divided into five parts. The two parts near the body form a universal joint, which allows the leg to move in all directions. At the end of the leg there are tiny spurs which allow the butterfly to cling to perches and flowers. Butterflies have very sensitive taste sensors on their legs.

Butterfly Leg

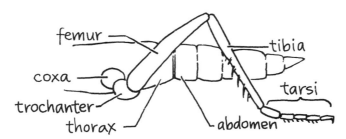

The abdomen is the last and softest part of the body. It contains ten to eleven segments with six or seven pairs of breathing spiracles on the sides. The external reproductive organs are found in the last three segments. On some butterflies, the auditory sense organs are located at the end of the abdomen.

Experiences

- Initial Observation: Gather the children in small groups to view the butterfly. Hopefully the first observation will be when the butterfly is emerging from its chrysalis. Record the children's comments and questions on a Butterfly Observation class chart.

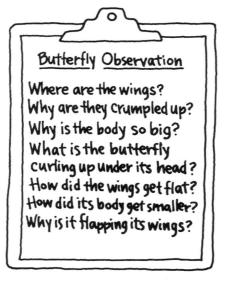

If the first observation takes place several hours or a day after the butterfly has emerged from its chrysalis, the comments on the Butterfly Observation chart will be different.

- Pose questions to guide and extend the children's observations: *How do you think the butterfly got out of the chrysalis? How many wings can you see? Do they have the same colors on the top and bottom? Where are the wings attached? Where are the legs attached? How many legs can you see? Where is the abdomen? Where is the head? Can you find something curled up under the head? What do you think it is?*

- If children have not been able to observe the butterfly coming out of its chrysalis and going through the early changes, spend time looking at books together, examining and discussing photographs of newly emerged butterflies. Some particularly good photographs are found in *Butterfly & Moth* by Paul Whalley and *Life of the Butterfly* by Heiderose and Andreas Fisher-Nagel.

- Encourage children to visit the butterfly cage often on their own, to discuss their observations with their classmates.

- Have students record their thoughts, questions, and observations in writing and drawings in their journals or learning logs, or on one of the reproducible Observation Sheets provided in Appendix A. See the **Language Arts** section (Writing Experiences: Journals, Learning Logs, and Observation Sheets) for more details.

- Before formally looking at the butterfly again, review the comments and questions from the first group observation and children's independent observations. Then display the Butterflies Abound Poster.

  Help children relate their real-life butterfly observations to the labeled butterfly diagram. Discuss parts of the butterfly they might not have seen in order to expand their knowledge.

  Look at the classroom butterfly again so the students can view, discuss, and validate the new information and develop new questions. Add new comments and questions to the Butterfly Observation class chart.

- Discuss how the proboscis develops in two separate sections and is "zipped" together after the butterfly emerges from the chrysalis. See Background Information for details. Use a zipper to model how the hooks and spines join together.

- In order to observe the butterfly uncurl its proboscis for feeding purposes, you will need to provide a food source. It can be sugar water or flowers. Refer to a book containing information about your butterfly species or see the **Social Studies** section (Butterfly Gardening) for appropriate flower choices. To make a sugar solution, use 20% white sugar and 80% water, or 5–10% fructose and 90–95% water. Soak a cotton ball with the sugar solution and place it in a secure spot near the butterfly.

- To demonstrate how a butterfly's proboscis uncurls and curls, hold a paper "party blower" (sold as birthday party favors) upside down and blow. Then read the poem "Butterfly Tongues" by Aileen Fisher in *In the Woods, In the Meadow, In the Sky.* (See Bibliography.) Children can make Party Blower Butterflies. See the **Art** section (Butterflies) for directions.

- If available, look at dead butterfly specimens with the naked eye, with hand lenses, and microscopes. Identify anatomical parts.

- Remove some scales from a butterfly wing. If the butterfly is alive, gently brush some scales off the wing near the outer edge in order to avoid crippling the butterfly. Place the scales on a slide and view them under a microscope. Make an observational drawing of what is seen in a journal or on one of the reproducible Observation Sheets provided in Appendix A.

- Discuss the two ways wing scales produce color: through pigment and through scale structure. Explain that the structure of some scales produces colors in a manner similar to the way a prism produces color. Hold a prism in direct sunlight and produce colors. Let the children experiment with the prism afterwards.

- Look at photographs of magnified wing scales. Some good sources include *Butterflies and Moths* by Barrie Watts, *The Butterfly in the Garden* by Paul and Mary Whalley, *Monarch Butterflies* by Emilie Lepthien, and *Life of the Butterfly* by Heiderose and Andreas Fischer-Nagel.

- Look at "Butterfly ABC" in *Sesame Street Magazine,* Jan.–Feb., 1991 or the Butterfly Alphabet Poster. The photographs were taken by Kjell B. Sandved. Each letter of the alphabet is formed by the color patterns of the butterfly wing scales. See the Bibliography for information about ordering the poster.

- Discuss the anatomy of the wings and compare the wing construction to a sandwich. Make the following "sandwich" to help the children visualize the wing's structure. The chitin is the "bread." Cut two sheets of clear acetate in the shape of a wing. The veins are the "sandwich filling." The veins can be formed from flexible tubing such as plastic tubing, wire, licorice, or pipe cleaners. The model can be taken a step beyond the sandwich model by adding scales to the outer surface of each piece of "bread". Paint glue on the acetate and then sprinkle it with glitter or confetti to simulate scales.

- Continue entering data on a life cycle graph. See the **Math** section (Graphing) for suggestions.

- Make and label observational drawings of the butterfly for a life cycle chart, puzzle, spinner, or mobile. See the **Art** section (Life Cycle) for details.

- Measure the wing span of your class butterfly. See the **Math** section (Graphing) for more information and related activities.

- Review butterfly body parts as you sing "Butterfly Connections" to the tune of "Dem Bones." Words are provided in the **Music** section.

- Enjoy the following finger plays, poems, and chants. Words are provided in the **Language Arts** section.

  Finger Plays: "Butterfly Wings," "Two Little Butterflies," "Fragile Butterflies"

  Poems: "Butterfly" by John Gay, "The Little Butterfly," "A Butterfly," "I Can Spell," "My Butterfly," "Bickery Bickery, Bye"

  Chants: "Stamp, Stamp, Stamp," "Fly Away"

- Read some of the butterfly poems listed in the Bibliography.

  "Butterfly Tongues" by Aileen Fisher in *In the Woods, In the Meadow, In the Sky*

  "Butterflies" by Eve Merriam in *Fresh Paint*

  "Polly saw a butterfly" by Jack Prelutsky in *Beneath a Blue Umbrella*

  "The Butterfly" by Clinton Scollard in *Read-Aloud Rhymes for the Very Young*

- Encourage children to create original poems, songs, and stories inspired by their chrysalis observations and experiences. See the **Language Arts** section for suggestions (Writing Experiences: Poetry, Books).

- Look at photographs of a variety of butterflies found in reference books.

- Observe and discuss the symmetrical patterns on the wings of various butterflies. Activities for developing and extending an understanding of symmetry are suggested in the **Math** section (Symmetry) and in the **Art** section (Butterflies).

- Try some of the other experiences exploring variety in wing shapes and patterns offered in Science: Concept 5 (Variety).

- Use a computer graphic program to draw an imaginary butterfly. Details are offered in the **Math** section (Computer Science).

- Make butterfly pictures and sculptures from a variety of materials. Encourage children to observe the class butterfly closely and to include as many anatomical details as possible.

  Display the Butterflies Abound Poster as added reference. See the **Art** section (Butterflies) for ideas.

- Act out butterfly behaviors and movements. See **Physical Activities** ("Fluttering Butterflies") and **Dramatic Play** (Movement) for suggestions.

- Do cooking projects with a butterfly theme. See the **Cooking** section.

- Read nonfiction books about butterflies. See the Bibliography for some recommended titles.

- Read fiction books about butterflies.

  * *Amanda's Butterfly* by Nick Butterworth
  * *Remember the Butterflies* by Anna Grossnickle Hines
  * *The Lamb and the Butterfly* by Arnold Sundgaard
  * *The Butterfly Hunt* by Yoshi
    The Butterfly Ball and the Grasshopper's Feast by Alan Aldridge
    I Like Butterflies by Gladys Conklin
    Hi Butterfly by Taro Gomi
    Butterfly Time by Alice E. Goudey
    Darkness and the Butterfly by Ann Grifalconi
    The Blue Butterfly by Ned O'Gorman
    An Invitation to the Butterfly Ball by Jane Yolen

  See the Bibliography and the **Language Arts** section (Reading Experiences) for more information. An asterisk (*) before a book title means that specific Experiences suggestions for that book are offered in the **Language Arts** section (Reading Experiences).

  Create a Readers Theatre script for *An Invitation to the Butterfly Ball* by Jane Yolen or adapt Eric Carle's *The Very Busy Spider* into a script entitled *The Very Busy Butterfly.* See the **Language Arts** section (Readers Theatre) for ideas.

NOTES

What do you need in order to raise a butterfly?

What do caterpillars and butterflies eat?

Do butterflies die in the winter?

How does the Monarch know how to get to Mexico if it's never been there before?

I never see butterflies outside around here. Why not?

Concept 3: BASIC NEEDS and BEHAVIORS

Each stage of a butterfly (egg, caterpillar, chrysalis, and butterfly) needs certain conditions in order to develop. Each stage has survival behaviors and adaptations that help it meet the challenges of its environment.

Background Information

Basic Needs of the Developing Insect

- As a butterfly develops, certain conditions are necessary in order for it to complete its life cycle. All stages need acceptable temperatures and weather. All stages need to be free of predators, mold, and bacteria.

- An egg needs to be fertilized.

- A caterpillar needs to hatch on or near its food source. Most caterpillars are "host specific" and will only eat one plant or plants in one family.

- A chrysalis needs to be suspended from a sturdy perch.

- A newly emerged butterfly needs to have a suitable perch from which to hang, with room to spread and dry its wings. A butterfly also needs plentiful nectar sources and the opportunity to mate.

Raising Butterflies in the Classroom

- Rearing butterflies in the classroom provides opportunities for the students to understand from firsthand observation and experiences some of the basic factors in butterfly survival.

- If students wish to find their own egg or caterpillar to rear, ask a local lepidopterist or a butterfly enthusiast for information about when and where a particular stage of a butterfly species can be found locally. Perhaps a knowledgeable person will be willing to accompany your class on a field trip to hunt for eggs or caterpillars. In order to locate the desired caterpillar, find out what plant it eats (the *larval host plant*) and learn to identify it. Signs of a caterpillar include nibbled leaves and *frass* (caterpillar droppings). You may be able to locate eggs on the host plant as well. Be sure to collect leaves or branches of the host plant so your class caterpillar will have a good supply of appropriate food. Without the host plant, the caterpillar will starve.

- Caterpillars and chrysalises can be ordered from the suppliers listed in Appendix C. Some come in kit form, including all necessary food and a caterpillar and/or butterfly cage.

- The caterpillar and the butterfly need housing. A cage can be made out of:
  - a cardboard box with screening or netting
  - cardboard circles and netting or plastic
  - a plant covered with netting
  - an aquarium with screening on the top

If a cardboard box is used, cover the bottom with a piece of cardboard cut to the exact size of the cage so that the caterpillars can't get lost in the cardboard flaps. Then cover the floor with newspaper so that the cage can be easily cleaned and kept free of caterpillar frass. Cut a hole in the side of the box and cover it with plastic wrap to create a window for viewing. Cover the top of the cage with netting or screening to allow for ventilation.

Butterfly Cages

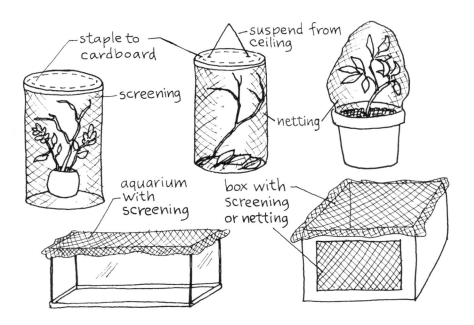

- Food for the class caterpillars is included in some commercial kits, such as the Painted Lady Butterfly Garden. However, for most other class caterpillars, the appropriate food must be provided by you and your students. For some caterpillars, the food source must be found locally in gardens and fields, for example, milkweed for the Monarch. For other caterpillars, the food can be purchased at a nursery, garden shop, or supermarket, for example, parsley and/or dill for the Black Swallowtail. A list of food sources for some common caterpillars is provided in the **Social Studies** section (Butterfly Gardening).

- Stalks or branches of the larval food source may be placed in a vase or other water container and kept in the caterpillar's cage. If you choose to do this, either cover the top of the water container and stick the end of the branches through holes cut in the cover, or stuff paper towels around the branches so the caterpillar does not fall into the water and drown.

- Butterflies will sip nectar from a variety of flowers, but many have preferred nectar sources. If the favored flowers are not readily available, mix a 20% white sugar, 80% water solution. Saturate a cotton ball or paper towel with the sugar water and place it in the cage.

Feeding Behaviors

- Most caterpillars are "host specific" which means they will eat only one kind of plant, or plants belonging to one specific family. Because butterflies lay their eggs on or near the specific food source, the chance for a caterpillar's survival is greatly increased. In general, caterpillars eat foliage, buds, and flowers. Some are carnivorous and eat aphids.

- Butterflies exercise a preference in nectar sources but are not as choosy as the "host specific" caterpillars. Butterflies eat nectar, tree sap, rotting fruit, dung, carrion, and water. It appears that butterflies also need salts. They get the salts by drinking at mud puddles (damp mud, sand, salt, gravel, etc.).

- Butterflies locate their food by scent and sight. They taste with their feet and eat (sip) with their proboscis, which works like a drinking straw. As a butterfly sips nectar, pollen from the flower often gathers on its body. As it sips from the next flower, grains of pollen may fall off its body, pollinating the second plant. In this way, butterflies help maintain the availability and growth of their favored plants.

Reproductive Behaviors

- During their short lives, butterflies need to mate in order to produce offspring. The male butterfly finds a female through scent and visual recognition.

- Butterflies do a courtship dance. A typical dance is as follows: The butterflies circle each other and beat their wings. The male's forewings touch the female's antennae. This contact releases sex scents (pheromones) from the androconia scales on the male's wings. The scents excite the female. The butterflies face in opposite directions, the ends of their abdomens touching. The male deposits sperm in the female. Later, the sperm will fertilize the eggs as they are laid.

- In order for butterflies to mate in the classroom, you must have a male and a female butterfly of the same species. In some species, males and females can be identified by their different markings or coloring.

Survival Behavior Related to Weather and Seasonal Changes

- Because a caterpillar or butterfly's body temperature is regulated by the temperature of its environment, weather and seasonal changes greatly affect its chance for survival.

- Temperatures that are too hot (127° F) or too cold (30° F) can kill a butterfly.

- Low temperatures can delay the development of an egg or chrysalis from several days to several weeks.

- Butterflies usually do not fly unless the sun is out. The air temperature must be warm enough to heat up their wing muscles. The optimal temperature for the flight of most butterflies is about 78° F, although they will fly in temperatures as low as 60°. Butterflies usually don't fly on cloudy days. Scientists think this may be because they sense that a storm may arrive, or it may be because butterflies rely on the sun for directional orientation clues, and without it become confused.

- Butterflies have developed different ways of coping with daily fluctuations in weather and seasonal changes. Some behaviors include:

    diapause - similar to hibernation in vertebrates, diapause is a period of inactivity or dormancy during cold, harsh weather. Commonly called *overwintering*.

    aestivation - dormancy during hot or dry periods

    migration - moving from one region to another

- In America, the Monarch butterfly is famous for its migration. In Europe, Cabbage Whites, Red Admirals, Clouded Yellows, and Painted Ladies migrate on a limited scale.

- Different species of butterflies overwinter in different stages of development. Some examples are listed on the following chart.

How Butterflies Overwinter

egg	*larva*	*pupa*	*butterfly*
bronzes	admirals	American copper	American Painted Lady
most coppers	checkerspots	American Painted Lady	Buckeye
	fritillaries	Painted Lady	Comma
	Hackberry	Red Admiral	Monarch
	satyrs	Spring Azure	Mourning Cloak
	Tawny Emperor	swallowtails	Painted Lady
	Viceroy	whites	Question Mark
			Red Admiral
			West Coast Lady

- Information about survival behaviors and adaptations related to predators is provided in Science: Concept 4 (Protective Behaviors).

Preserving Butterfly Habitats

- Construction, deforestation, and environmental pollution have had grave effects on butterfly populations. Information is provided in the **Social Studies** section (Butterfly Conservation).

- Conservation experiences in the **Social Studies** section suggest ways students can learn about and participate in efforts to protect butterfly habitats and attract more butterflies to their area.

Experiences

Raising Butterflies in the Classroom (Providing for Basic Needs)

- Make plans to purchase or find the stage of the butterfly you wish to raise. This can include writing a letter requesting a caterpillar or chrysalis, going on a field trip to find one, or receiving a caterpillar or chrysalis from some other source.

- Discuss the requirements of a caterpillar/butterfly cage. Even if your class kit comes with a butterfly cage, your students may enjoy researching various designs for homemade cages and making one to replace the commercial cage or making individual cages for their own home use.

- The following books and article provide information and instructions for building caterpillar/butterfly cages and providing for their needs:

    It's Easy to Have a Caterpillar Visit You by Caroline O'Hagan

    How to Raise a Butterfly by E. Jaediker Norsgaard

    Sally's Caterpillar by Anne and Harlow Rockwell

    Terry and the Caterpillar by Millicent Selsam (Note: Terry hatches a moth, but the book is appropriate.)

How to Raise the Monarch Butterfly by Sally Spooner

Caterpillar and *Butterflies and Moths* by Barrie Watts

"Grow Your Own Butterfly" by Elizabeth Shaver in *Cricket,* July 1991.

- Discuss and list what is needed for survival during each stage of the butterfly's development.

Basic Needs of a Developing Butterfly

- Acceptable temperatures
- No mold or bacteria
- Fresh air
- No predators

Needs to be fertilized.	Needs to eat particular plants.	Needs a sturdy perch.	Needs a place to hang and dry its wings and needs to sip nectar.

- Discuss the fact that most caterpillars are "host specific;" they will eat only one type of plant or plants belonging to one specific family. If students plan to find their own caterpillar, have them do research to find out its particular food source. If the class caterpillar has come in a kit with a processed food source, students can do research to find out what type of plant leaves were ground up and packaged. The field guides and butterfly gardening books listed in the Bibliography provide information about caterpillar food preferences. A chart listing the larval food sources of a number of common butterfly species is also included in the **Social Studies** section (Butterfly Gardening).

- Obtain plenty of fresh food for your class caterpillar. Without the appropriate food source, the caterpillar will die. Place the locally found food, or the commercial caterpillar food, in the caterpillar's cage. Leaves can be kept fresh by placing the stalks or branches in water; however, students must safeguard against the danger of the caterpillar falling in the water and drowning. Let students brainstorm and propose solutions. Some options are suggested in the Background Information (Raising Butterflies in the Classroom).

- Students can care for the egg, caterpillar, chrysalis, and butterfly. Their responsibilities will include keeping the cage clean, especially of caterpillar frass, and keeping the caterpillar or butterfly well fed.

- Celebrate the release of your class butterfly with finger plays, chants, songs, stories, and other festivities.

  Finger plays: "Fragile Butterflies," "A Chrysalis" (see **Language Arts** section)

  Chant: "Fly Away" (see **Language Arts** section)

  Songs: "The Butterfly Dance" (see **Music** section)
  "Lovely Butterflies" by Stephen Titra, "Butterfly" by Susan Bamel (see Bibliography)

- Read *The Lamb and the Butterfly* by Arnold Sundgaard and *The Butterfly Hunt* by Yoshi. Share the wordless picture book, *Amanda's Butterfly* by Nick Butterworth. These books gently remind children of the butterfly's right to fly free. The **Language Arts** section offers ideas for extending children's involvement with these books.

- Make snacks related to the butterfly theme. See the **Cooking** section for recipes.

NOTES

Feeding Behaviors

- If the class is rearing a caterpillar, put both its preferred food source and another food source in the cage. Observe the caterpillar. Does it go near the other food source? Does the caterpillar taste and reject it or ignore it completely?

- Discuss where butterflies lay their eggs and how this gives the caterpillars a better chance for survival.

- Read *The Very Hungry Caterpillar* by Eric Carle. Discuss what the caterpillar ate in the story. Engage the students in a discussion of caterpillar food preferences by posing the following questions:

    Do you think real caterpillars eat any of the foods the Very Hungry Caterpillar ate? Do you have favorite foods? Do all caterpillars/butterflies like the same food? Does anyone know a caterpillar or butterfly that likes a particular food?

    See the **Dramatic Play** and the **Language Arts** sections (Books and Readers Theatre) for additional ideas for extending children's involvement with this book.

- If you are providing your caterpillar with fresh food, record and graph the amount it eats each day. See the **Math** section (Graphing) for more information.

- Make a chart of caterpillar and/or butterfly food preference. Children and teachers can do this research in conjunction with butterfly reports. Information about food preference can be found in the **Social Studies** section of this Guide (Butterfly Gardening), and in butterfly field guides and butterfly gardening books listed in the Bibliography.

Species	Caterpillar's Preferred Food	Butterfly's Preferred Nectar
Monarch	milkweed	aster milkweed
Eastern Black Swallowtail	wild carrot, dill, parsnips (carrot family)	thistle milkweed
Buckeye	plantain snapdragon	aster chicory

- Using the food preference chart created above, write and illustrate a poem based on "Fragile Butterfly." The poem and activity description are provided in the **Language Arts** section (Writing Experiences: Poetry, Innovated Poems).

- Learn about butterfly gardening. If possible, start seedlings for children to take home and plant, or plan and plant a butterfly garden near the school. See the **Social Studies** section (Butterfly Gardening) for information about plants that attract specific butterfly species and other gardening tips.

- Enjoy the following poems and chants. Words and teaching suggestions are provided in the **Language Arts** section:

  Poems: "The Little Butterfly," "A Butterfly," "Everywhere"

  Chants: "Caterpillars Eat," "Who Ate My Food?" "Stamp, Stamp, Stamp"

- Read the following poems:

  "Caterpillars" by Aileen Fisher in *Cricket in the Thicket* or *Surprises*

  "Butterflies" by Leland Jacobs in *Just Around the Corner*

  "Polly saw a butterfly" by Jack Prelutsky in *Beneath the Blue Umbrella*

  For more information see the Bibliography (Poetry).

- Sing the song "Caterpillars" to the tune of "Frere Jacques." The words are found in the **Music** section.

- Make snacks related to the butterfly and caterpillar feeding behaviors theme: "Nectar" and "Caterpillars on a Leaf." Recipes are provided in the **Cooking** section.

NOTES

Reproductive Behavior

- If possible, identify the sex of the classroom butterflies. *An Instant Guide to Butterflies* by Pamela Forey and Cecilia Fitzsimmons and *Butterflies and Moths* by Robert Mitchell and Herbert Zim contain relevant information for some species.

- If you have several class butterflies of the same species, including a male and female, keep them together with an ample supply of nectar or sugar water and fresh, healthy branches of the caterpillar host plant, and you may be able to observe mating behavior and egg laying.

- Discuss the importance of a butterfly finding its mate quickly due to its short life span. Describe the butterfly courtship dance. (See Background Information.)

- Look at close-up photographs and read information about mating behaviors and egg laying which can be found in several of the nonfiction books listed in the Bibliography, including:

  The Life of the Butterfly by David Drew (Big Book)

  The Life Cycle of the Butterfly by Paula Hogan

  The Butterfly Life Cycle by Oxford Scientific Films

  Butterfly & Moth by Paul Whalley

  The Butterfly in the Garden by Paul and Mary Walley

  Swallowtail Butterflies by Jane Dallinger and Cynthia Overbeck

- Help students create a Readers Theatre script based on Eric Carle's book *The Very Busy Spider*. The Readers Theatre script can be entitled, "The Very Busy Butterfly." Suggest that the butterfly be very busy laying eggs. See the **Language Arts** section (Readers Theatre) for ideas on developing and performing the script.

NOTES

Survival Behaviors Related to Weather and Seasonal Changes

- Find Monarch caterpillars in the fall or order them from a supplier (see Appendix C). Watch the caterpillars pupate and emerge, then release the butterflies, allowing them to migrate south.

- Read *Where Do Butterflies Go When it Rains* by May Garelick to stimulate discussions about what butterflies and other animals do when the weather changes.

- Discuss and chart different ways animals cope with weather changes. Ask the children to think of an animal and what it does to protect itself from cold, heat, rain, or dry spells.

Weather	Animal	Behavior
cold	bear	eats, grows thick coat, hibernates
cold	most birds	migrate

- Ask the children how they think butterflies spend the winter.
  Where do you think butterflies go in the winter? How do they survive the cold weather? In which stages of development do you think butterflies spend the winter?

  Encourage children to make predictions based on their knowledge of other animals. Record their responses on a chart.

- Once the children have probed the question of how butterflies survive the winter, read sections of books containing information. One source is: *Where Do They Go? Insects In Winter* by Millicent Selsam (pages 21–25).

- Discuss butterfly *diapause* (overwintering or hibernation), *aestivation*, and *migration* with the children. See Background Information.

- Read about Monarch migration:

  Monarch Butterfly by Gail Gibbons

  The Great Butterfly Hunt by Ethan Herberman

  Wanderer: The Monarch Butterfly by Don Hoffman

  The Travels of Monarch X by Ross Hutchins

  The Butterflies Come by Leo Politi (fiction)

  "My Mexican Monarchs" in *Ranger Rick,* October 1991

- Use a globe and/or maps in an atlas to trace where Monarchs migrate. See the **Social Studies** section (Geography) for more information.

- Find out how the class butterfly and other butterflies overwinter. If children are researching different butterflies the information can be organized on a class chart.

How Different Butterflies Overwinter	
Monarchs	butterfly (migrates)
Swallowtails	chrysalis
Coppers	egg
Tawny Emperors	caterpillar

- Read the following poems:

    "About Caterpillars" by Aileen Fisher, in *When It Comes to Bugs*

    "Butterflies Dancing Through Falling Snow" by Demaru, in *Eric Carle's Animals Animals*

    "Caterpillar, Caterpillar" by Helen Fletcher, in *Finger Play Poems and Stories*

- Sing the song "Winter Time" to the tune of "Where, Oh Where Has My Little Dog Gone?" The words are provided in the **Music** section. Encourage the students to create new verses about the overwintering behaviors of different butterfly species.

- Do an experiment to see if daily temperature affects the length of time it takes for a chrysalis to develop. If possible use two chrysalises that formed on the same day. Place one in the refrigerator (not freezer) for 3–4 days and leave the other at room temperature. Compare the amount of time that the two chrysalises take to become butterflies. (Do not use chrysalises that are overwintering in the chrysalis state.)

- If there is a butterfly habitat nearby, visit often to find out at what temperature the butterflies become active. Students can develop a form to record the information and use this data to develop theories about the effects of temperature on flight. Students can record their data and thoughts in journals, learning logs, or on charts.

NOTES

Preserving Butterfly Habitats (Providing Basic Needs)

- Discuss how construction and pollution have destroyed butterfly habitats. Information is provided in the **Social Studies** section (Butterfly Conservation).

- Have students speculate about how destruction of habitats and pollution have affected the survival of butterfly species. Write questions and comments on a chart:

> ## What's Happening to the Butterflies?
>
> What would happen if all the butterflies died?
>
> I don't see any butterflies around my house.
>
> Did there used to be more butterflies here?
>
> How can we get more butterflies to live here?

Refer to the related experiences in the **Social Studies** section (Butterfly Conservation; Butterfly Gardening).

- Find out what local species of butterflies are endangered. Discuss what actions could be taken to increase their chances of survival. Contact conservation agencies for information. Students may enjoy writing a play about Butterfly Conservation incorporating their new knowledge. They can present their play to various audiences. See the **Social Studies** section (Butterfly Conservation) for more suggestions.

- Read the poem "Hurt No Living Thing" by Christina Rossetti. The poem is printed in the **Language Arts** section.

NOTES

Do caterpillars and butterflies have enemies?

How do they protect themselves?

Why is our caterpillar so fuzzy?

Why are butterfly wings different colors underneath?

Why do lots of butterflies have big spots on their wings?

If a bird bites off a piece of a butterfly's wing, will it die?
Will the butterfly still be able to fly?

Concept 4: PROTECTIVE BEHAVIORS

Each stage of a butterfly (egg, caterpillar, chrysalis, and butterfly) has behaviors and adaptations that help it escape predators.

Background Information

At all stages of its life a butterfly has predators. The **eggs** are eaten by beetles, lacewings, bugs, snails, and parasitic wasps. **Caterpillars** are attacked by ants, wasps, lacewing larvae, and birds. **Chrysalises** are preyed upon by lizards, birds, and parasites, and **butterflies** are food for birds, spiders, dragonflies, wasps, bugs, lizards, frogs, toads, and small mammals.

Butterflies have impressive methods of defense against their predators. Among these survival behaviors and adaptations are:

Good vision - Butterflies quickly see approaching enemies.

Evasive flight - Butterflies escape danger by using evasive flight techniques: zig-zag patterns, dropping to the ground, etc.

Mimicry - Some tasty butterflies resemble distasteful ones. They escape being eaten because they look like the unpalatable species. An example of this is the nonpoisonous Danaid eggfly which resembles the poisonous Tiger butterfly. Some scientists believe that the Viceroy butterfly is a palatable species which mimics the bad-tasting Monarch. Other scientists believe that both the Viceroy and the Monarch are bad-tasting. For more information on this controversy, read page 39 of "Delicious or Deadly?" in *The Great Butterfly Hunt* by Ethan Herberman.

False targets - Many butterflies and caterpillars have large decorative circles near their tails. These "eye spots" attract predators and make them strike there rather than at more vital spots, such as the head. Sometimes the "eye spots" scare enemies away—perhaps because they are mistaken for the eyes of a much larger animal. Hairstreak butterflies have conspicuous tails as well as spots on their hind wings, making their back ends look like their heads.

Camouflage - The color and/or the shape of the egg, caterpillar, chrysalis, and butterfly often helps the insect blend in with its surroundings. Caterpillars, chrysalises, and butterflies sometimes resemble twigs, dead or living leaves, seed pods, thorns, or bird droppings.

Flash coloration - The front wings of some butterflies are dull colored, blending with the colors of their surroundings, while the hind wings are bright and colorful. If attacked, these butterflies flash their hind wings to startle the predator, then dart away.

Posture changes - Some caterpillars rear up and frighten off predators.

Feigning death - Some caterpillars and butterflies "play possum."

Concealment - Some caterpillars wrap themselves in a leaf during the day and eat at night. Others spin a silken web around a leaf and hide within so as not to be seen.

Night feeding - Some caterpillars, especially those that are grass feeders, avoid their predators by hiding close to the ground during the day and feeding only at night.

Dazzling/Eclipsing - Many butterflies have bright colors on the top surface of their wings and dull, camouflage colors underneath. These butterflies use their contrasting wing colors to confuse and evade enemies. First, the butterfly opens its wings, dazzling the predator with the bright colors, then it quickly raises and closes its wings, seemingly disappearing as the colors blend in with the surroundings.

Defensive odors - Some caterpillars, such as the swallowtails, have an *osmeterium* which, when erect, gives off an offensive odor. Other butterflies, such as the zebras, also have a bad smell.

Spines and prickly hairs - Some caterpillars and eggs have hairs that are irritants to predators or simply unappetizing.

Bright coloration - Bright colors warn predators that the butterfly or caterpillar is poisonous or not tasty.

Experiences

- Discuss the different protective behaviors of various animals. Chart the children's responses.

Think of an animal with which you are familiar. What does it do to protect itself against its enemies?

Animal	Protective Behavior
cat	hisses and scratches
bear	attacks and runs
oppossum	plays dead
chameleon	runs; changes colors to blend in with surroundings (camouflage)

Then ask children to think about protective behaviors butterflies may use. Again, chart the children's responses.

How do you think the egg, the caterpillar, the chrysalis, and the butterfly defend themselves against their enemies?

Protective Behaviors			
Egg	Caterpillar	Chrysalis	Butterfly
camouflage located where not easily seen	camouflage concealment furry, unappetizing body	camouflage	camouflage fly away

- The learning experiences suggested below will help children explore specific behaviors that help butterflies escape predators.

- To find out more about protective behaviors and adaptations, read appropriate sections in books such as the following:

  Discovering Butterflies & Moths by Keith Porter

  Butterflies and Moths by James P. Rowen

  Backyard Insects by Millicent E. Selsam

  Amazing Butterflies and Moths by John Still

  Butterfly & Moth by Paul Whalley

  The Butterfly in the Garden by Paul and Mary Whalley

- When children have participated in the learning experiences and have discussed the defensive behaviors and adaptations of butterflies, review the class chart of Protective Behaviors. Ask the class to add any new information.

Good vision

- Locate a butterfly and observe it from afar. Slowly get closer to the butterfly, then make a sudden movement. The butterfly will see you, sense danger, and fly off.

Evasive flight

- Watch the flight of as many different kinds of butterflies as possible. Describe and imitate their flight patterns (zigzag, gentle glide, fast and whirling, rapid flight with sudden stops, etc.).

- After watching its flight, chase after a butterfly as if you were going to catch it. Notice what happens to its flight pattern and what it does to escape from you, its predator.

- Sing "Butterfly Dance" to the tune of "Frere Jacques." Words are provided in the **Music** section.

- Read the poem "Butterflies" by Eve Merriam in *Fresh Paint*. For more information, see the Poetry section of the Bibliography.

- Act out the finger play "Butterfly Wings." The words are provided in the **Language Arts** section.

Mimicry

- Make two batches of popcorn or any other food appropriate to the activity. Salt one batch heavily. Lightly salt and generously butter the other batch. Offer the heavily salted batch first. Ask who wants a second portion. This time give out the other batch. Hopefully many children will turn down the second batch assuming it will taste like the first. Relate this popcorn eating activity to a predator eating a distasteful butterfly or caterpillar and then avoiding another similar-looking yet different kind of butterfly.

Camouflage

- Cut a green sponge into a long strip, dampen it with water and sprinkle it with grass seeds or seeds that germinate easily and quickly. Keep the sponge wet, warm and in sunlight so the seeds will germinate. Once the seeds have sprouted, the sponge will look like a green, hairy "caterpillar." Ask the children what would be the best place for this "caterpillar" to live if it wished not to be seen. Discuss and demonstrate the concept of camouflage. Place the sponge caterpillar in the suggested spots and see where it is camouflaged best.

- Read *How to Hide a Butterfly and Other Insects* by Ruth Heller. See the Bibliography for more information.

- Show pictures of different eggs, caterpillars, chrysalises, and butterflies and discuss where they might be best camouflaged.

- Have a class hunt. Show and then hide about six objects in places that provide camouflage possibilities. The hunt can be timed. When it is over, repeat the procedure but place the objects where they do not blend with the surroundings but rather are in sharp contrast. Compare and discuss the difficulty of the two hunts.

- Read the poem "Caterpillar" by Christina Rossetti. The poem is printed in the **Language Arts** section. Discuss how the caterpillar in the poem protects itself from its predators, the toads and the birds.

- Play "Butterfly Tag." See the **Physical Activities** section for details.

Defensive odors

- Choose several odoriferous items, some edible and some inedible. Place each item on a cotton ball, wrap it with cheesecloth, and place it in a can or jar with holes in the lid. Possible items could include onion, vanilla, lemon, soap, and poster paint. Be sure to avoid items that might cause allergic reactions. Have children sniff the containers and decide which items smell good enough to eat.

Spines and prickly hairs

- Bring foods to school that could be described as spiny, hairy, or smooth, such as artichokes and coconuts, apples and mangoes. Judging by outward appearances only, discuss which foods look palatable and which do not. Relate this experience to a bird choosing whether to eat a hairy or a smooth-skinned caterpillar.

NOTES

How many kinds of butterflies are there?

How large is the largest butterfly?

How small is the smallest butterfly?

Do male and female butterflies look different?

How did different butterflies get their names?

Are the different swallowtails cousins?

Concept 5: VARIETY and CLASSIFICATION

The eggs, caterpillars, chrysalises, and butterflies of different species display a great variety of colors, shapes, and sizes. Scientists classify butterflies into groups according to various attributes.

Background Information

There are about 20,000 species of butterflies worldwide. Tropical rain forests are the most heavily populated butterfly habitats. About 700 butterfly species are found in North America. An enormous variety of shape, color and size can be found among the different species and within each stage of the life cycle.

An excellent way to help children become knowledgable about and appreciate the diversity among butterflies is to raise two or more butterfly species and to observe and compare them. Reading about different species and looking at a wide variety of pictures of different species in their different stages is also helpful.

When trying to identify a butterfly in any of its stages, consider the following:

appearance - color, shape, size, pattern

geography - location, elevation

habitat - swamp, meadow, woodland, grasslands, mountains

food source - caterpillars and butterflies will usually be found in areas where their larval and nectar sources grow

time of year

Learning about the characteristics of families and subfamilies will also help you identify specific butterflies.

Butterflies are classified according to differences in their form and structure. They are grouped into families according to differences in:

- the shape of wings
- the pattern of veins in the wings
- the wing coloration
- leg peculiarities
- mouth parts
- position and shape of the eyes
- other features, such as genitals

Butterflies are divided into two superfamilies. The Hesperioidea, "the skippers," tend to be stocky, compact, and hairy. They have short triangular wings that are usually brown, black, gray, or tawny orange. The Papilionidea, "the true butterflies," tend to have narrow bodies, long antennae, and brightly colored full wings. They are further divided into families and subfamilies.

The Butterfly Classification Chart in Appendix B contains the families and common names of some of the well-known butterflies in North America. Scientists do not always agree on how to classify butterflies. Some subfamilies on this chart will be listed as families on other charts.

Taxonomists are scientists who study the system of grouping living things. Their job includes identifying, naming, and grouping newly found animals and plants. Every animal and plant has a two-part scientific name. The first name indicates the genus, the second name indicates the species. The names are usually Latin or Greek in origin. In this book, common names rather than scientific names are used.

Some butterflies have been given their common names because of appearance: Mourning Cloak, Tortoise Shell, Yellow Tiger Swallowtail, Hairstreaks. Some have been named after their larval host plant: Hackberry Butterfly, Anise Swallowtail. Still others are named for their color: Blues and Whites.

Experiences

- Raise two or more different butterfly species in the classroom. Have students observe and compare the species as they go through their life cycle changes. A comparative chart can be created, recording the data collected through observation and reading.

- If you have only one type of butterfly in the classroom, use this as the model to which other butterflies can be compared. Observe, describe, and draw each stage of the butterfly's development, then compare with other species pictured and described in books.

- Eggs. Look at classroom egg (if this stage is available) and at drawings and photographs of eggs of different butterfly species. Have students observe carefully, ask questions, and make comments. Discuss similarities and differences. Draw pictures of different butterfly eggs. Label and display.

Brainstorm a list of butterfly egg characteristics. Create a chart, web, or narrative with the information. Then, circle the words that describe the characteristics of the class butterfly egg.

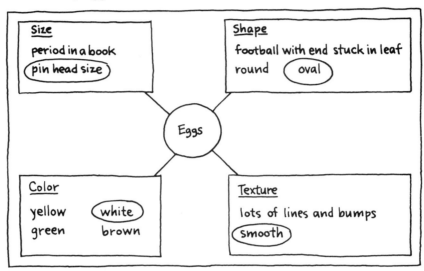

- Caterpillars. Look at the classroom caterpillar and at drawings and photographs of caterpillars of different species. Have students observe carefully, ask questions, and make comments. Discuss similarities and differences.

Brainstorm a list of caterpillar characteristics. Create a chart, web, or narrative with the information.

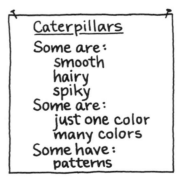

Have the children identify caterpillars that have color patterns. The children can describe the pattern ("It has a yellow band around its body with lots of black dots then a black band with three big yellow dots and then it's repeated"). Use art materials such as beads, blocks, clay, paint, markers, or crayons to reproduce the patterns seen or to create imaginary ones. See the **Art** section (Caterpillars) and the **Math** section (Sequencing) for more ideas.

- Chrysalises. Look at the classroom chrysalis and at drawings and photographs of chrysalises of different species. Have the students observe carefully, ask questions, and make comments. Discuss similarities and differences. Draw pictures of different chrysalises. Label and display.

  Brainstorm a list of chrysalis characteristics. Create a chart, web, or narrative with the information.

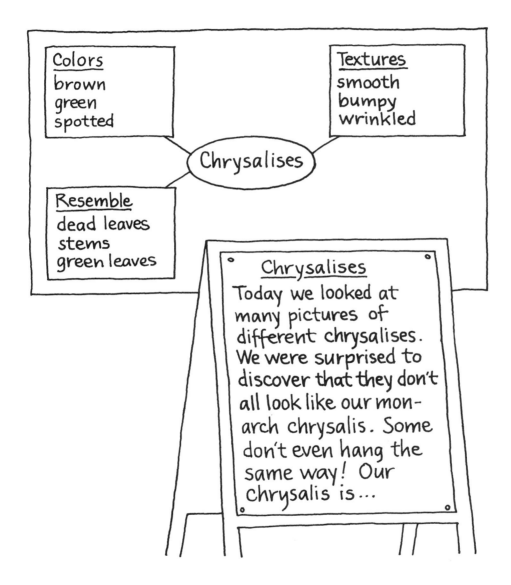

- Butterflies. Look at the classroom butterfly and at drawings, photographs, and specimens of butterflies of different species. Have the children observe carefully, ask questions, and make comments. Discuss similarities and differences.

  Brainstorm a list of butterfly characteristics. Create a chart, web, or narrative with the information.

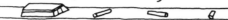

```
                              Butterflies
    Colors                            Shapes (Wings)
    - have all colors                 - upper wings pointy
    - some one color                  - upper wings round
    - some many colors                - bottom wings round
    - some are bright                 - bottom wings with 1 "tail"
    - some are dull                   - bottom wings with 2 "tails"

    Wing Designs                      Size
    - same on both sides(symmetrical) - as big as dinner plates
    - some have big spots             - as small as dimes
    - veins help make designs         - the size of a soup can lid
```

Use art materials to recreate specific butterflies or to invent imaginary ones. See the **Art** section (Butterflies) for specific ideas.

- Read books about specific butterfly species.

Monarchs

Monarch Butterfly by Gail Gibbons
The Great Butterfly Hunt by Ethan Herberman
Wanderer: The Monarch Butterfly by Don Hoffman
The Butterfly by Paula Z. Hogan
The Travels of Monarch X by Rosse Hutchins
Nature's Children, Monarch Butterfly by Bill Ivy
The Monarch Butterfly by Judith Josephson
Monarch Butterflies by Emilie U. Lepthien
Life Cycle of a Monarch Butterfly by Julian May
How to Raise the Monarch Butterfly by Sally Spooner

Swallowtail Butterflies

Butterflies by Althea Braithwaite
Butterfly by Michael Chinery
Swallowtail Butterflies by Jane Dallinger and Cynthia Overbeck.
The Swallowtail Butterfly by Oda Hidetomo
Where Butterflies Grow by Joanne Ryder

Cabbage Whites

The Life of a Butterfly by David Drew (Big Book)
Butterfly and Caterpillar by Barrie Watts
The Butterfly Life Cycle by Oxford Scientific Films

Peacock Butterflies

Life of the Butterfly by Heiderose and Andreas Fischer-Nagel

- Have groups of children research the life cycle of more than one kind of butterfly. Gather field guides and books with clear photographs to demonstrate diversity among butterflies. Individuals or groups of students can research different butterfly species and present reports to the class. The reports may be in the form of charts, books, or life cycle posters. Students can cooperatively create wall charts or Big Books describing a number of different species. See the **Language Arts** section for ideas (Writing Experiences: Books, Reports).

- As part of their report on a particular butterfly species, students can shade in the area where their butterfly lives on a blank outline map. See the **Social Studies** section (Geography) for more information.

- Make life cycle time lines or time wheels for different butterfly species. Compare the amount of time different species spend in each stage of development. See the **Math** section (Graphing) for details.

- Make wing span graphs, comparing the wing spans of different species. See the **Math** section (Graphing) for ideas.

- The South American rain forest is home to a very large number of butterfly species. The destruction of the rain forest is threatening many of them with extinction. Encourage students to find out about some of the butterfly species living in the rain forest and to learn about efforts to save their habitat. See the **Social Studies** section (Butterfly Conservation) for related information and ideas. Children may enjoy making a Rain Forest Butterfly Mural. See the **Art** section (Butterflies) for details.

- Collect duplicate pictures of various caterpillars and butterflies. Use the pictures to make and play matching games such as lotto, concentration, or dominoes. See the **Math** section (Classifying) for other game variations.

- Read *I Like Caterpillars* and *I Like Butterflies* by Gladys Conklin.

- Read *Discovering Butterflies* by Douglas Florian. See the **Language Arts** section (Reading Experiences) for additional experiences with this book.

- Read the poems "Caterpillars" and "My Butterfly." The poems are found in the **Language Arts** section. Encourage students to create their own versions of the poems. Make the original versions into poem posters or Big Books.

- Sing the song "Do You Know the Butterflies?" The words are provided in the **Music** section.

- Teach the song "A-Hunting We Will Go." The words are provided in the **Music** section. Children can create additional verses naming different butterflies. Write the words to the verse on a chart. Instead of writing the name of a butterfly on line 4, place a piece of velcro in the empty space. Prepare strips of oak tag to fit in this space. Place a piece of velcro on the back of each strip. Students can create new verses by naming different butterflies. Help students write the name of the chosen butterfly on a strip and attach it to the chart. Then sing the new verse with the class.

If you wish, mount pictures of familiar butterflies on cards and place velcro on the backs. Put a piece of velcro on the song chart. Let children create verses by attaching a matching butterfly name strip and picture card to the chart.

- Review or introduce the chants, "Caterpillars Eat" and "Who Ate My Food?" The words are provided in the **Language Arts** section.

- Write poems about the characteristics of particular butterflies. Children can create acrostic poems, haiku, patterned poems (original verses based on existing poems), tongue twisters, or free verse. See the **Language Arts** section for detailed suggestions (Writing Experiences: Poetry).

- Make drawings of a wide variety of caterpillars and butterflies. Use the drawings to make Big Books titled *We Like Caterpillars* and *We Like Butterflies*. See the **Language Arts** section for more details (Writing Experiences: Books).

- *The Icky Bug Alphabet Book* by Jerry Pallotta may inspire students to create a Butterfly ABC book, featuring a different species for each letter of the alphabet. See the **Language Arts** section for more information (Writing Experiences: Books).

- The following butterfly zoos provide rare opportunities for children to see a wide variety of living butterflies. If you live near any of these areas, try to arrange a field trip.

* Butterfly World in Coconut Creek, Florida, is about ten miles from Fort Lauderdale.
* Butterfly World at Marine World Africa USA is in Vallejo, California, about 35 miles from San Francisco.
* Day Butterfly Center at Callaway Gardens, Pine Mountain, Georgia, is about 30 miles from Columbus and 65 miles from Atlanta.
* Papillon Park in Westford, Massachusetts, is about 40 miles from Boston.

• Enlarge the classification chart found in Appendix B. Discuss the chart with the children. Read some of the particularly descriptive names, asking the children what they think the butterfly might look like. Use a field guide to show pictures of the butterflies you discuss. You may wish to focus on the characteristics of one butterfly family or subfamily each day.

• Create a class Big Book, each page featuring student-generated information and pictures about the *Butterfly of the Day*. See the **Language Arts** section (Writing Experiences: Books) for more details.

• If a student is researching a particular butterfly, have him or her find out to which family it belongs. When the student shares the report, he or she can post a labelled photograph or drawing next to butterfly's name on the classification chart. As pictures or drawings accumulate, children may develop an understanding of the distinctive characteristics of different families.

• For more ideas on ways to help students develop reports on different butterfly species, see the **Language Arts** section (Writing Experiences: Reports).

• Look at the poster "Butterflies" produced by American Teaching Aids (ATA), which has drawings of butterflies grouped by families. See the Bibliography for ordering information.

• Collect pictures of many different butterflies. Pictures can be cut from field guides, magazines, calendars, wrapping paper, etc. These pictures can be classified according to various attributes:

   butterflies with smooth-edged wings
   butterflies with wavy-edged wings
   butterflies with larger upper wings
   blue butterflies, yellow butterflies, etc.

Two good sources for pictures are the photographs in the *Audubon Society Pocket Guide: Familiar Butterflies* and Carol Belanger Grafton's set of 87 authentically detailed drawings found in *Butterfly Stickers in Full Color*. Both can be purchased from Papillon Distributors, Inc. See the Bibliography and Appendix C for more information.

• Students can pretend to be taxonomists and classify pictures of eggs, caterpillars, and chrysalises by their characteristics—colors, patterns, coverings, etc.

- Reproduce the butterfly drawings in Appendix A. Use these outline drawings to examine and discuss the variety of wing shapes. Let children develop ways to group the butterflies, for example:

  wings with "tails" vs. wings without "tails"
  forewings larger than hind wings vs. forewings about the same size as hind
    wings
  wavy edges vs. no wavy edges

  See the **Math** section (Classifying) for more information.

NOTES

LANGUAGE ARTS

When children are involved in a thematic inquiry they use a variety of language skills such as reading, writing, listening, and speaking to share their ideas, gather information, pose questions, and solve their problems. In this way they are developing important communication skills within the context of meaningful content. The language arts become avenues for learning more about the topic, butterflies.

In the Language Arts section we have provided a wealth of suggestions for enjoying and exploring literature while building a richer understanding of the concepts being developed in this theme study. The experiences have been organized into the following sections:

Finger Plays, Poems, and Chants

Starting the day with a warm-up of butterfly fingerplays, chants, poems, and songs sets a mood of community, enjoyment, participation, and focuses creative energy. Write the chants and poems on chart paper to facilitate the shared reading experience. Often children enjoy composing original verses following the pattern set in the original poem or chant. Fingerplays, poems, and chants provide special opportunities to enjoy the images and rhythm of language. Body movements, percussive accompaniment, and varied use of voices (group or solo, high or low, fast or slow) can add new dimensions to oral reading.

Big Books and Trade Books

Enthusiastic involvement with books is a key feature of our approach to learning. We have incorporated a large number of fiction and nonfiction books into our Guide. Some are in Big Book form, most are regular size and available in many libraries. In this section we first offer some general ideas for enhancing students' experiences with books, then suggest specific learning experiences for seventeen selected book titles. We hope these suggestions will serve as helpful models as you and your students devise ways of extending and enjoying your own favorite books.

Readers Theatre

A Readers Theatre script transforms a book into a play with characters and narrators reading assigned lines. Poems or scripts written by children also often lend themselves to a Readers Theatre performance. This section provides sample scripts and offers suggestions for creating other Readers Theatre scripts with your students.

Writing Experiences

Throughout this theme study, students record their observations, experiences, thoughts, questions, and newly acquired information. Writing experiences are also an integral part of students' involvement with poetry and books. This portion of the Language Arts section offers a wide selection of different forms of writing that students can explore for enjoyment, expression, and as an important tool for learning.

FINGER PLAYS, POEMS, and CHANTS

Finger Play Experiences

- Finger plays offer students a playful opportunity to practice oral language, dramatic expression, creative movement, and motor skills. Finger plays lend themselves to singing, choral reading, and reading in assigned parts.

- Introduce a finger play by reciting it or reading it aloud. Demonstrate the gestures. Then invite students to join in. Display a chart or a transparency with the words of the finger play written in large print. Read the text aloud, pointing to the words. Gradually encourage students to take over this "teacher role."

- After the children have become familiar with a finger play, they may enjoy making finger puppets, stick puppets, or flannel board figures and acting out the verses.

Some of the finger plays in this section are adapted from traditional sources; others we have written ourselves.

Butterfly Wings (adapted from a traditional finger play)
SCIENCE CONCEPTS 2 and 4: Metamorphosis; Protective Behaviors

I have four little wings	*(hold out two fingers on each hand)*
And they all belong to me.	
I can make them do things.	
Would you like to see?	*(wiggle the fingers)*
I can put them together tight	*(close fingers)*
Or open them wide.	*(open fingers)*
I can make them flutter,	*(flutter fingers)*
Or rest them side by side.	*(rest fingers)*
I can use them to fly high.	*(move fingers high)*
I can use them to fly low.	*(move fingers low)*
I can fold them quietly	*(rest fingers together)*
And hold them just so.	

The Caterpillar (adapted from a traditional finger play)
SCIENCE CONCEPT 2: Metamorphosis

A caterpillar crawled to the top of a tree	(right fingers crawl)
"I think I'll take a nap," said he.	(fingers sideways)
So onto a stem he began to creep,	(fingers crawl in reverse direction)
To make his chrysalis	(wiggle body)
And to fall asleep.	(fingers rest)
All winter he slept, all snug in his bed	(fingers rest)
Till spring came along one day and said,	(left hand lifts)
"Wake up, wake up, little sleepy head!	(left hand waves)
Wake up, it's time to get out of bed!"	
So he opened his eyes that sunshiny day	(join hands at thumbs
Lo! He was a butterfly and flew away!	and wiggle fingers)

Two Little Butterflies (adapted from a traditional finger play)
SCIENCE CONCEPT 2: Metamorphosis

There were two pretty butterflies	(hold up two fingers)
Resting on a flower,	(rest two fingers on palm of other hand)
One named Rosa	(lift one finger)
The other named Gower.	(lift second finger)
Fly away Rosa,	(hand flies away)
Fly away Gower.	(hand flies away)
Come back Rosa,	(hand flies back)
Come back Gower.	(hand flies back)

Fuzzy Wuzzy Caterpillar
SCIENCE CONCEPT 2: Metamorphosis

Fuzzy wuzzy caterpillar	
Onto a stem it crept	
Into a chrysalis it turned	(turn around)
And for a long time it slept.	(head in hands)
Fuzzy wuzzy caterpillar	
Wakened by and by	(stretch)
Emerged with such graceful wings;	
A beautiful butterfly.	(flutter arms)

One Little Egg
SCIENCE CONCEPT 2: Metamorphosis

One little egg   *(hold one finger up)*
Sitting all alone,
Out comes a caterpillar   *(wiggle finger)*
Oh, how it's grown!
Next it will rest   *(lay finger in opposite palm)*
We all know why.
Soon it'll come out a butterfly!   *(with hand up, wave fingers)*

Fragile Butterflies
SCIENCE CONCEPTS 2 and 3: Metamorphosis; Basic Needs

Butterflies are fragile things
Fluttering daintily with their wings.   *(lock thumbs and wiggle)*
Floating, gliding in the sky
I'm a graceful butterfly!   *(raise locked hands
                                         higher, higher)*

Fuzzy Little Caterpillar (adapted from Emilie Poulssen's 1893 fingerplay)
SCIENCE CONCEPT 2: Metamorphosis

Fuzzy little caterpillar,
Crawling, crawling on the ground,   *(move fingers forward)*
Fuzzy little caterpillar,
Nowhere, nowhere to be found,
Though we've looked and looked
    and hunted   *(hands to eyes)*
Everywhere around!   *(look around)*

When the little caterpillar
Found its furry coat too tight,   *(hug self)*
Into a chrysalis it turned,
Covered with skin so thin and light;
Transforming itself within,   *(roll hands)*
It slept there day and night.   *(palms together, rest head)*

See how this chrysalis is stirring!   *(swing fist back and forth)*
Now a little head we spy—   *(poke thumb out of fist)*
What! Is *this* our caterpillar
Spreading gorgeous wings to dry?   *(lock thumbs together;
Soon the free and happy creature   flutter fingers)*
Flutters gaily by.   *(make "butterfly" fly)*

A Chrysalis

SCIENCE CONCEPT 2: Metamorphosis

Here is a chrysalis hanging from a tree. *(right hand between other thumb and pointer finger)*

Something is moving *(hand to ear)*
Let's wait and see.
See it wiggle out, wings folded tight, *(touch thumbs, fingers folded down)*

Spreading them open, ready for flight . . . *(spread fingers)*
A flittering fluttering butterfly.
There it goes flying—wave goodbye! *(wave hands)*

NOTES

Poetry Experiences

On the following pages we have provided a number of traditional and original butterfly poems that we have enjoyed using with our students. In addition, we have enjoyed using many authored butterfly poems. These poems are referred to within the **Science** and **Social Studies** sections under Experiences. They are also listed in the Bibliography, indexed by the anthologies in which they are found. We hope you are able to gather some of these excellent poems to share with your class.

- To introduce a poem, write the words on a large chart or on a transparency. Read the poem aloud, enjoying the sounds and rhythms of the language. Read it again, pointing to the words as you read and encouraging children to join in.

- With the children, experiment with different ways of reading each poem. Poems can be read chorally, or they can be divided into parts for groups or solos. Vary the tempo, the voice pitches and volumes to enhance the interpretation of the piece. Encourage children to add gestures for dramatic emphasis. Rhythmic clapping and drums can reinforce the sound or language patterns of a poem.

- Make a tape of butterfly poetry for your Listening Center. Record a variety of readers—parents, students, the whole class, yourself—reading and reciting favorite poems. Provide printed copies of the poems so students can read along as they listen to the tape.

- Reproduce poems you have introduced in class on individual sheets. Children can illustrate their favorite poems and take them home to share with their families. Children can choose their favorite poem to memorize and perform for the class.

- Particular lines or verses of a favorite poem can be printed on posters or pages to create a wall chart or a Big Book that children can illustrate.

- Using the basic structure and language pattern of a poem, individuals and groups can create their own adaptations or add new verses.

- Cloze and masking techniques can be used with poem charts. Cover words or parts of words with removable tape or self-stick removable notes. Students use clues of meaning, word order, and sound to predict the hidden word. This masking technique can also be a strategy to encourage students to insert their own words into the structure of a poem, creating an original "innovated" piece.

Caterpillar
by Christina Rossetti
SCIENCE CONCEPT 4: Protective Behaviors

Brown and furry
Caterpillar in a hurry,
Take your walk
To the shady leaf, or stalk,
Or what not,
Which may be the chosen spot.
No toad spy you,
Hovering bird of prey pass by you;
Spin and die,
To live again a butterfly.

The Butterfly by John Gay
SCIENCE CONCEPT 2: Metamorphosis

"And what's a butterfly?
At best, he's but a caterpillar,
    dressed."

The Little Butterfly
SCIENCE CONCEPT 3: Basic Needs

I saw a little butterfly
By the hickory tree
He was sipping nectar
And wouldn't look at me.

Hurt No Living Thing
by Christina Rossetti
SCIENCE CONCEPT 3: Basic Needs

Hurt no living thing;
Ladybird, nor butterfly,
Nor moth with dusty wing,
No cricket chirping cheerily,
Nor grasshopper so light of leap,
No dancing gnats, nor beetle fat,
Nor harmless worms that creep.

A Butterfly
SCIENCE CONCEPT 3: Basic Needs

Brightly colored butterfly
Looking for a flower
Spread your wings and fly away
To a garden bower.

I Can Spell
SCIENCE CONCEPT 2: Metamorphosis

I can spell c-a-t-e-r
I can spell p-i-l-l-a-r
I can spell caterpillar.

I can spell b-u-t-t-e-r
I can spell f-l-y
I can spell butterfly!

Everywhere

SCIENCE CONCEPT 3: Basic Needs

Caterpillars, caterpillars everywhere
Crawling here
Climbing there
Eating cabbage
Munching parsley
Caterpillars, caterpillars everywhere.

Butterflies, butterflies everywhere
Flying over coral bells
Fluttering by goldenrod
Sipping nectar
Eating juices
Butterflies, butterflies everywhere.

Caterpillars

SCIENCE CONCEPT 5: Variety

We like caterpillars
Fuzzy caterpillars
Smooth caterpillars
Small caterpillars
Long caterpillars
Striped caterpillars
Spotted caterpillars
All kinds of caterpillars
We like caterpillars.

Anywhere they are
Climbing up a tree
Chewing on a leaf
Crawling on the grass
Anywhere they are
We like caterpillars.

Fuzzy Wuzzy

SCIENCE CONCEPT 5: Variety

Fuzzy wuzzy was a caterpillar
Fuzzy wuzzy had lots of fur
Fuzzy wuzzy was very fuzzy,
wasn't he?

Can You?

SCIENCE CONCEPT 2: Metamorphosis

Can an egg
    climb up a leg
    play mumblety-peg
    eat nutmeg
    kneel and beg
No . . . but an egg can become a caterpillar.

Can a caterpillar
    be a burglar
    or a lawyer
    eat a frankfurter
    hold a hammer
No . . . but a caterpillar can become a chrysalis.

Can a chrysalis
    play tennis
    eat an amaryllis
    handle a crisis
    climb a trellis
No . . . but a chrysalis can become a butterfly.

What can you do?

This Little Caterpillar *(adapted from the traditional rhyme)*
SCIENCE CONCEPT 2: Metamorphosis

This little caterpillar went to market
This little caterpillar stayed home
This little caterpillar ate green leaves
This little caterpillar ate none
And this little caterpillar turned
        into a chrysalis on her way home.

Little Miss Muffet *(adapted from the traditional rhyme)*

Little Ms. Muffet
Sat on her tuffet
Eating her curds and whey
Along came a caterpillar
Who crawled by to thrill her
And frightened Miss Muffet away.

Five Little Caterpillars
SCIENCE CONCEPT 2: Metamorphosis

Children can make finger puppets, or decorate the five fingers on a glove to look like caterpillars, then let the "caterpillars" act out the following poem.

Five little caterpillars creeping without a sound
The first little caterpillar crawling round and round
The second little caterpillar munching on a leaf
The third little caterpillar crawling up a sheaf
The fourth little caterpillar no longer very thin
The fifth little caterpillar shedding his skin.

My Butterfly
SCIENCE CONCEPTS 2 and 5: Anatomy; Variety

Scales painted with pastels
Delicate lines of each wing
Woven like pretzels
Salted with spots.

Bickery Bickery Bye

Bickery Bickery Bye.
A butterfly flew up in the sky
The boy in brown
Tried to get him down
Bickery Bickery Bye.

NOTES

Chant Experiences

- Copy the chants on chart paper or make a transparency for shared reading. Demonstrate the text by reading it aloud several times, pointing to the text as it is read. Then, invite the children to join in chorally.

- Assign lines or verses to individuals, partners, or groups according to the format of the chant. Use your voices theatrically—different volumes, pitches, and speeds can be used for emphasis and to create different moods. Rhythm instruments can reinforce the beat. Children can create hand or body motions to accompany the words.

- Tape record the children as they recite a favorite chant and place the tape in the listening corner with a read-along copy of the text. Provide each student with a small take-home copy of the chant to illustrate and share with his or her family.

- With your students, create a Big Book version of a favorite chant. Write sections of the chant, a verse or a few lines, in enlarged print on each page. Let children illustrate the book. Your class Big Books can become a permanent part of your class or school library.

- The written text provides opportunities for word study within a meaningful context. Pose questions that get students to focus on particular phrases, words, or sounds. For example, ask students to find a word they know, a word that begins with the same letter as their name, a word with an "ed" ending, or a word that means almost the same as another given word. The students can place a window or mask, made from a piece of cardboard, over the word to frame their response. These questions should vary according to the needs and understandings of the students.

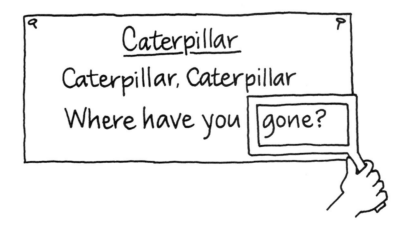

- Use the cloze technique to encourage students to use clues of meaning, word order, and sound to predict unfamiliar words. Cover words or parts of words with removable tape or self-stick removable notes. Have students guess the hidden words and discuss the clues that support their prediction.

- Sometimes a chant lends itself to "innovation." To "innovate" new verses, substitute new words or phrases into the basic pattern of the chant. If you wish, adapt the cloze technique as a strategy to encourage student innovations. Cover key words and phrases on the chant chart with strips of paper or self-stick removable notes. Let students suggest or write new words on these strips, creating new verses to the chant. Your class may enjoy using these innovated verses as the text for an original class Big Book.

The Arabella Miller Chant

SCIENCE CONCEPT 2: Metamorphosis

This chant is an adaptation of the song "Little Arabella Miller" found in the Music section. It can be read chorally, or sung to the tune of "Twinkle, Twinkle, Little Star."

Chorus:	Little Arabella Miller Had a fuzzy caterpillar.
Reader 1:	It crawled upon her daddy's cap While he was taking a nap.
Chorus:	Little Arabella Miller Had a fuzzy caterpillar.
Reader 2:	It crawled upon her mother's nose Just as she started to doze.
Chorus:	Little Arabella Miller Had a fuzzy caterpillar.
Reader 3:	It sneaked upon her brother's clothes And then snuggled between his toes.
Chorus:	Little Arabella Miller Had a fuzzy caterpillar.
Reader 4:	It climbed along her sister's knee And made her cry hysterically.
Chorus:	Her family said "Arabella Miller Get rid of that caterpillar!"

What Do You Get?

SCIENCE CONCEPT 2: Metamorphosis

This two-sided chant can be read by partners, one reading the first two lines of each verse and the second reading the remaining lines. Or the parts can be assigned to two groups of students.

Eggs are laid by chickens.
What do you get?
> A chick.

Eggs are laid by turtles.
What do you get?
> A turtle.

Eggs are laid by alligators.
What do you get?
> An alligator.

Eggs are laid by butterflies.
What do you get?
> A caterpillar...
> then a chrysalis...
> and finally,
> a beautiful butterfly!

Now what do you think of that!
> Now what do you think of that!

Who Ate My Food?

SCIENCE CONCEPTS 3 and 5: Basic Needs; Variety

This question-answer chant can be read by partners or two groups of students. As students learn what various caterpillars eat, they can add new verses.

Who ate the leaves from the milkweed plant?
> "I", said the Monarch in a soft, squeaky voice.

Who ate the parsley from my garden green?
> "I", said the Swallowtail in a raspy voice.

Who ate the thistle from my garden bed?
> "I", said the Painted Lady in a soft little voice.

Caterpillars Eat

SCIENCE CONCEPTS 3 and 5: Basic Needs; Variety

This chant can be read by partners or two groups, one reading the first line, and the other responding with the second. As students learn the eating habits of different caterpillars, they can add new verses.

A Monarch likes to eat milkweed.
I like to walk or skip full speed.

A Painted Lady likes to eat thistle.
I like to swim and blow my whistle.

A Buckeye likes to eat a snapdragon.
I like to go downhill with a red wagon.

A Black Swallowtail eats Queen Anne's lace.
I like to run in a very long race.

A Viceroy likes to eat lots of willows.
I like to toss fluffy pillows.

A Spring Azure eats meadowsweet.
I like to walk in my bare feet.

A Red Admiral likes to eat nettles.
I like to make music with fine kettles.

Birth of a Butterfly

SCIENCE CONCEPT 2: Metamorphosis

This chant lends itself to part reading or echo reading.

Egg, egg, where have you gone?
      I've turned into a caterpillar
      crawling on your lawn.

Caterpillar, caterpillar, where have you gone?
      I've turned into a chrysalis
      Still, quiet, but not for long.

Chrysalis, chrysalis, where have you gone?
      I've turned into a butterfly
      on this beautiful morn.

Stamp, Stamp, Stamp

SCIENCE CONCEPTS 2 and 3: Metamorphosis; Basic Needs

This chant can be read in unison, or parts can be assigned to individuals and groups: the boy, the butterflies, and the narrator.

Stamp, stamp, stamp went the butterflies' feet.
"What are you doing?" asked a boy of the beat.
"We're tasting, we're tasting this flowery treat."
"What? Tasting, tasting with your long skinny feet?
That's hard to believe; I use my tongue, not my feet."

Fly Away

SCIENCE CONCEPTS 2 and 3: Metamorphosis; Basic Needs

This chant can be sung to the tune of "Five Little Chickadees." Five students can read the first verse, four can read the second verse, three can read the third verse, and so on. Five other students, perhaps using puppets, can act out the countdown story. All students can read or sing the choral refrain.

Five little butterflies fluttering by the door
One flew away and then there were four.
>Butterfly, butterfly, happy and gay,
>Butterfly, butterfly, fly away.

Four little butterflies resting on a tree
One flew away and then there were three.
>Butterfly, butterfly, happy and gay,
>Butterfly, butterfly, fly away.

Three little butterflies playing around you
One flew away and then there were two.
>Butterfly, butterfly, happy and gay,
>Butterfly, butterfly, fly away.

Two little butterflies fluttering in the sun
One flew away and then there was one.
>Butterfly, butterfly, happy and gay,
>Butterfly, butterfly, fly away.

One little butterfly having lots of fun
It flew away and then there were none.
>Butterfly, butterfly, happy and gay,
>Butterfly, butterfly, fly away.

NOTES

BIG BOOKS AND TRADE BOOKS

- Read aloud to your students every day, sharing many types of literature. Throughout this Guide we have recommended a wide range of books in both Big Book and trade book sizes to help extend students' knowledge of various aspects of butterfly study and to offer literary enjoyment. Be sure to include both fictional and nonfictional books in your read-aloud repertoire.

- Engage students as active participants in the read-aloud experience. Encourage them to connect their personal knowledge to the new text as they talk about the title and the cover illustration. Ask them to make predictions about the story. As you read the story aloud, stop at various points, raise authentic questions, and let students voice their questions. Encourage focused discussion and ask for more predictions. As you continue to read, the questions may be answered and the predictions confirmed or disproved.

- Big Books offer special opportunities for shared literacy experiences. As you read the Big Book aloud, point to the text to demonstrate print concepts. Invite students to join in with the reading when they are ready. The large illustrations in Big Books often provide an excellent focus for group discussion.

- In later readings of the Big Book, use cloze and masking techniques with the words. Cover words or parts of words with removable tape and strips of paper, or self-stick removable notes. Students can use clues of meaning, word order, and sound to predict the hidden word. Pose questions that get students to focus on particular phrases, words, or sounds. For example, ask students to find a word they know, a word beginning with the same letter as their name, a word with an "ed" ending, or a word that means almost the same as another given word. The students can place a window or mask, made from a piece of cardboard, over the word to frame their response. Vary your questions according to the needs and understandings of the students.

- If a trade book has a repeated refrain, you may want to write these words in large print on a chart. Invite students to read the words or chant along each time they repeat in the text.

- Read favorite books together many times, until students have internalized the story. A variety of cross-curricular activities can grow out of the literature experience once it becomes an old favorite.

- Many Big Books can be reread with part-reading. Children can assume the roles of the various characters. Other children can read the narration. Trade books can also often be adapted into Readers Theatre script. For more information, see the Readers Theatre section of this **Language Arts** section.

- Record yourself, a parent, or a child reading a favorite book. Place the tape at the Listening Center, along with a copy of the book.

- The cloze technique, described above, can be used as a strategy to help students create an original "innovated" version of a Big Book story. Have students suggest new characters, events, and descriptions to insert into the structure of the story.

- Make small sized versions of a favorite book for each child to illustrate and take home to read. Use the original text or a version that the class has created through "innovation."

On the following pages, we suggest specific learning experiences for the following fiction and nonfiction books. We hope these suggestions will serve as helpful models as you and your students devise ways of extending and enjoying your own favorite books.

LANGUAGE ARTS

Big Books

The Very Hungry Caterpillar by Eric Carle
Caterpillar Diary by David Drew
The Life of the Butterfly by David Drew
Sometimes Things Change by Patricia Eastman
The Longest Journey in the World by William Barrett Morris

Trade Books

Amanda's Butterfly by Nick Butterworth
Charlie the Caterpillar by Dom DeLuise
The Life of the Butterfly by Heiderose and Andreas Fischer-Nagel
Discovering Butterflies by Douglas Florian
Monarch Butterfly by Gail Gibbons
Remember the Butterflies by Anna Grossnickle Hines
I Wish I Were a Butterfly by James Howe
Where Butterflies Grow by Joanne Ryder
Amazing Butterflies and Moths by John Still
The Lamb and the Butterfly by Arnold Sundgaard
The Butterfly Hunt by Yoshi

BIG BOOKS

The Very Hungry Caterpillar by Eric Carle
SCIENCE CONCEPTS 2 and 3: Metamorphosis; Basic Needs

- This predictable book offers students a delightful story paired with vivid illustrations. In common with many other books, poems, and songs, this book erroneously refers to a butterfly emerging from a *cocoon*. Ask the students to see if they can identify the mistake the author made on the final pages of the book. Reread the pages. If the students wish, the correct word, *chrysalis*, can be taped over the word *cocoon*.

- Students can create an innovated version of the story, suggesting new foods that the caterpillar can eat. Create a class Big Book using this innovated text. Have students illustrate each page. You may want to use the page design from the book, each page (Monday–Friday) being a little wider than the preceding page. Punching a hole in each food illustration (that students can poke a finger through) also adds interest.

- To focus on days of the week, color words, food words, or number words, cover words with gummed removable note paper, or strips of paper and removable tape. This will encourage students to make predictions using the story context.

- Students can retell *The Very Hungry Caterpillar* story and write the major events on sentence strips. They can then sequence the strips, placing them in a pocket chart. Put the pocket chart and sentence strips in a Learning Center with a copy of the book. The children can independently practice rereading and re-sequencing the sentence strips.

- Individuals or groups of students can also use the pocket chart, sentence strips, and blank word cards to create innovated versions of *The Very Hungry Caterpillar*. The students can write a word on a blank card and place it over the word that they wish to change.

- Using masks (see Big Book and Trade Book Experiences), have students identify various words and create large charts to classify them. The following are some examples:

Words that tell Where
around
inside
through

Days of the Week
Sunday
Monday

Number Words
one
two
three

Words that tell About	
One	Several
apple leaf	pears plums

Fruits	Meats	Sweets
apple pear banana	salami sausage	chocolate cake ice cream

Compound Words
cupcake watermelon

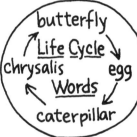

Describing Words
cherry chocolate beautiful

- Children can create a caterpillar puppet using a single finger cut from a glove. Have students draw a picture of a food their caterpillar likes to eat on a piece of oak tag. Help them cut a hole through the middle of the picture, and poke the caterpillar through the opening. The caterpillar can be attached with tape or glue so the child can wiggle a finger through the opening.

Front

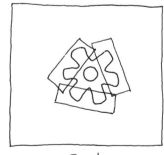

Back

A class book can be made of a series of these food pages. A single caterpillar can be glued or taped to the back of the book, and can protrude through all the pages of the book.

- Construct a large graph of the foods the Hungry Caterpillar ate. The students can color in a box or record their name to show which of these foods is their favorite. Total the columns and discuss the results.

- Students can re-enact what the Hungry Caterpillar ate by having apples for snack on Monday, pears on Tuesday, etc.

- Make a list of the foods the Hungry Caterpillar ate. Circle those foods that some real caterpillars eat. See Science Concept 3: Basic Needs (Feeding Behaviors) and the **Social Studies** section (Butterfly Gardening) for more information.

- Act out *The Very Hungry Caterpillar*. See the **Dramatic Play** section for details.

Caterpillar Diary by David Drew
SCIENCE CONCEPT 2: Metamorphosis

- Read aloud *Caterpillar Diary*, a Big Book by David Drew. Stop to examine and discuss the magnificent close-up photographs and the charts on the final page and back cover. Help students note that this book depicts the life cycle of a moth rather than a butterfly.

- Students can observe their own caterpillar and record daily pictorial observations in a journal or on one of the reproducible Observation Sheets provided in Appendix A. See the **Science** section (Concept 2) and Writing Experiences in this **Language Arts** section (Journals, Language Logs and Observation Sheets) for ideas for journal entries.

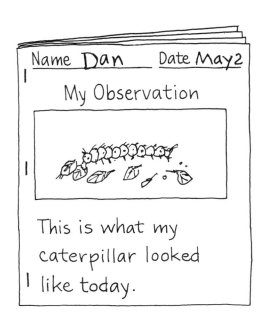

- Small group, partners, or individuals may wish to create a continuous chart to record their observations of the caterpillar. See the **Math** section (Graphing) and the **Art** section (Life Cycle) for suggestions on data students might enjoy collecting and recording.

Watching My Caterpillar		
Date	Length	Drawing
9/27	1"	
9/29	1¼"	

The Life of the Butterfly by David Drew
SCIENCE CONCEPT 2: Metamorphosis

- Read aloud *The Life of the Butterfly*, another excellent Big Book by David Drew. This life cycle book has a very interesting format. Four different elements are incorporated on each page: a close-up photograph, a brief explanatory text, a chart providing information about the butterfly in that particular stage (habitat, food, enemies, etc.), and an intriguing Mystery Fact, posed as a question for students to ponder. Thus, there are many ways for you to read this book. On the first reading you may wish to simply examine and discuss the photos and read the explanatory text. Or you may also want to read some, but not all of the Mystery Facts. Or you may wish to preview the format with the students and let them select a way for you to read. Or you can simply refer to the index to locate particular information of interest.

- As a small group, students can create their own series of pictures and charts based on a butterfly of their own choosing, using the format of this Big Book as a model.

- Students can compile and illustrate their own Mystery Facts book, adding other fascinating bits of butterfly knowledge. Or the class might enjoy sharing their theme study with the rest of the school by creating a Butterfly Mystery Facts hall display.

Sometimes Things Change by Patricia Eastman
SCIENCE CONCEPT 2: Metamorphosis

- Display and discuss the title and cover of the Big Book, *Sometimes Things Change*. Ask, *What are some of the ways things can change?* Read the book aloud, and then with the help of the students, create a chart listing the items described.

First	Then
caterpillar	butterfly
tadpole	frog
egg	turtle
grape	raisin

- Ask the students in small groups to brainstorm other things that change. Each group can then make assignments and create their own version of the book, *Sometimes Things Change*.

The Longest Journey in the World by William Barrett Morris
SCIENCE CONCEPT 2: Metamorphosis

- Before reading the Big Book, *The Longest Journey in the World*, ask students to imagine their backyard or a park and to think of objects or places a caterpillar might crawl over, under, or through. Record their responses on a chart.

  After reading the book, return to the pre-reading chart adding the column, "Might Look Like", and have the children decide what the objects in the first column might have looked like to a caterpillar.

Place	Might Look Like
hose	snake
rock	mountain

- Discuss with the children what might happen if a caterpillar crawled around the classroom. Begin a chart showing where the caterpillar might crawl and what it might look like from the caterpillar's perspective.

- Have students continue the brainstorming with a partner or small group; ask one student in each group to record the ideas on a chart. Each student can choose one place to illustrate, and a class Big Book, *The Day the Caterpillar Visited Our Classroom,* can be created for all to enjoy.

- Re-enact *The Longest Journey in the World,* using real props. See the **Dramatic Play** section for more information.

- Reread the Big Book, *The Longest Journey in the World.* Ask students to consider how the perspective may change when the caterpillar becomes a butterfly. Using the text as a model, create a class Big Book from the butterfly's perspective. It can begin:

  One sunny afternoon
  As I was flying around
  This is what I spotted
  Far below upon the ground

  I saw a . . . (ladybug crawling, children playing, an ant carrying food).

  The children can compose their own phrases and illustrate the scenes from the butterfly's perspective. These can be collated into a Big Book. The final page can show the butterfly resting on a flower, saying, "That was the longest journey in the world."

- Small typed copies of this innovated text will make wonderful little books for the children to illustrate, reread, and share with their families.

TRADE BOOKS

Amanda's Butterfly by Nick Butterworth
SCIENCE CONCEPT 3: Basic Needs

- Share *Amanda's Butterfly* with your students. This wordless picture book tells the story of a young resourceful girl named Amanda, who enjoys catching butterflies. One rainy day, she encounters a butterfly fairy with a damaged wing. The illustrations give the characters personality and clearly show the predicaments and the sequence of events.

- As the book is shared, young children will learn to tell the story by interpreting the pictures, paying careful attention to details. As they relate the story, write it on a chart, and then reread it with the class.

- As a follow up, students can draw a simple series of pictures to create their own wordless stories. You may want to share other wordless story books to help the students become more familiar with this genre. *Good Dog, Carl* by Alexandra Day is another wordless book children of all ages can enjoy.

Charlie the Caterpillar by Dom DeLuise
SCIENCE CONCEPT 2: Metamorphosis

- Read *Charlie the Caterpillar,* a story about true friendship, to your students.

- Discuss what true friendship means and have students share thoughts on how they can be good friends.

- Read and discuss other stories about friendship, such as *Amos and Boris* by William Steig. Compare the messages.

- Discuss the true meaning of "beauty." Have students compare this story to *I Wish I Were a Butterfly* by James Howe.

- After listening to *Charlie the Caterpillar,* children can respond by writing in their journals. Later they can share their written reactions to the story.

- This story lends itself to a puppet dramatization. After listing the important characters, students can decide what materials they will need to make the puppets, and who will make each puppet. Help the class form different casting groups, each group having a full set of story characters, and perhaps a narrator as well. Let the groups work cooperatively, making their puppets and practicing their performance. The groups can perform for each other or for other classes. For ideas on how to make puppets see the **Art** section (Life Cycle).

Life of the Butterfly by Heiderose and Andreas Fischer-Nagel
SCIENCE CONCEPTS 2, 3, and 5: Metamorphosis; Basic Needs; Variety)

- Read aloud the beautiful book, *Life of the Butterfly,* by Heiderose and Andreas Fischer-Nagel. It is filled with wonderful photographs of butterflies. In particular, it depicts the life cycle of a Peacock butterfly. It also discusses the behaviors of various butterflies. Point to the details in the photographs as appropriate.

- As the book is read, list the highlighted words such as family, species, Metamorphosis/Anatomy, brush feet, and claspers on a large chart so they can be reviewed and discussed after the completion of the book. There is an excellent glossary at the back of the book that can be used as a reference.

- You may want to create a class book or individual books about butterflies. Each child can choose a word from the chart, use it in a sentence or paragraph, and illustrate the idea conveyed. The word itself can be traced with a colored marker, and the collection of pages assembled in a book entitled *About Butterflies*.

- Another bookmaking option is to make a picture glossary, with each student designing a page. In a glossary, it is not necessary to have a word entry for each alphabet letter. There may be more than one entry for a letter.

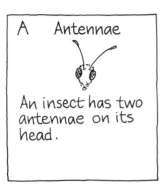

A   Antennae

An insect has two antennae on its head.

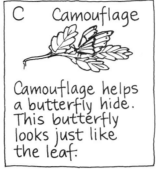

C   Camouflage

Camouflage helps a butterfly hide. This butterfly looks just like the leaf.

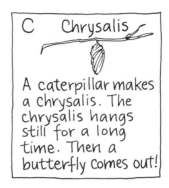

C   Chrysalis

A caterpillar makes a chrysalis. The chrysalis hangs still for a long time. Then a butterfly comes out!

Discovering Butterflies by Douglas Florian
SCIENCE CONCEPTS 2 and 5: Metamorphosis; Variety

- Read aloud *Discovering Butterflies,* examining and discussing the illustrations with the students. Each illustration includes a magnification marking (×1, ×8, etc.) indicating how many times the proportions have been enlarged. Note and discuss these markers and spend a while looking at the diagram of the butterfly on page 12.

- As the book is read, record on a large chart the names of the butterflies that are described.

Discovering Butterflies

Brimstone   Morpho
African Dry-leaf   White
Owl butterfly   Painted Lady
Tiger Swallowtail   Skipper
Apollo   Monarch
Map   Rajah
Copper   Blue
Sulphur

- Student partners can select one of these butterflies and create a poster with an illustration and a short written description. These posters can be displayed in the room or collated to form a class book, *Discovering Butterflies.*

Monarch Butterfly by Gail Gibbons

SCIENCE CONCEPTS 2, 3, and 5: Metamorphosis; Basic Needs; Variety

- Read aloud *Monarch Butterfly*, stopping at two or three appropriate points for students to predict what will happen. Read on to confirm or disprove the predictions.

- Discuss the sequence of the life cycle as described in the story. Help students create a large class chart, complete with pictures of each stage. The **Art** section (Life Cycle) provides various ideas for life cycle drawings.

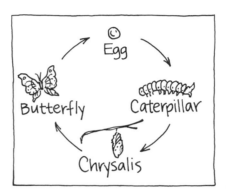

- The last section of the text includes a step-by-step guide to raising a Monarch butterfly. Using these instructions, the class may make a butterfly home, find and raise a Monarch caterpillar, watch it pupate and emerge, then finally release it. See the **Science** section (Concept 3: Basic Needs, Raising Butterflies) and the Bibliography for more information about caring for captive butterflies.

- Students can write daily journal entries and draw pictures to document their experience and their observation of the classroom Monarch. See the **Language Arts** section (Writing Experiences) for suggestions.

Remember the Butterflies by Anna Grossnickle Hines
SCIENCE CONCEPTS 2 and 5: Metamorphosis; Variety

LANGUAGE
ARTS

- Read *Remember the Butterflies* to your students. This story relates two children's memories of their grandfather, his tenderness and companionship, and his love and knowledge of butterflies. Discuss the ideas of "loss" and "memories" and "celebration" as it relates to Grandpa, his death, and what he taught the children.

- The book is filled with accurate information on the Spring Azure butterfly. The class can recall these facts and create a list or chart of information about this species.

- The life cycle of the butterfly can be related to the loss of life. Students may have their own stories of loss to share.

- This may naturally lead to personal writing. Students can write about a pet, a friend, or a family member they have lost and share their fond memories.

- You may want to introduce and discuss other books related to the theme of loss, such as *The Tenth Good Thing about Barney* by Judith Viorst.

I Wish I Were a Butterfly by James Howe
SCIENCE CONCEPT 1: Insects

- Read aloud *I Wish I Were a Butterfly* by James Howe, sharing the delicate, colorful illustrations by Ed Young with the students.

- Discuss how the cricket felt upon meeting each of the characters and how he changed when he was with the spider.

- Discuss what is meant by "beauty." Why do the students think the butterfly thought the cricket was beautiful?

- This story lends itself to a dramatic re-enactment. Students can choose a cast of actors, develop minimal props, arrange the set, then act out the story. To involve more actors, consider adapting the story to include a group of grasshoppers, butterflies, etc. instead of just one. When students have practiced the play and developed it to their satisfaction, they may invite other classes to their performance.

- The text of *I Wish I Were a Butterfly* can also be arranged into a Readers Theatre script. The Readers Theatre portion of this **Language Arts** section offers suggestions for creating a script.

The Caterpillar and the Polliwog by Jack Kent
SCIENCE CONCEPT 2: Metamorphosis

- Read *The Caterpillar and the Polliwog* aloud. This comical tale lends itself to many experiences. Record yourself reading the story and place the tape and a copy of the book in the Listening Corner for students to enjoy independently.

- Students can act out the story. After they have listened to the story several times, they will be able to ad-lib lines. Students can also create and perform a Readers Theatre script of the story.

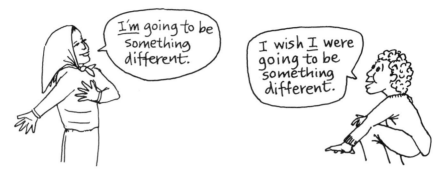

- Students can make stick puppets of the characters and use the puppets to dramatize the story.

- Provide materials for making flannel board figures. Have students use their figures to retell the story.

Where Butterflies Grow by Joanne Ryder
SCIENCE CONCEPTS 2 and 3: Metamorphosis; Basic Needs

- Display the cover of the book, *Where Butterflies Grow,* and ask students to describe the illustration. Encourage them to describe in detail the caterpillars and the Black Swallowtail butterflies. The students' comments can be recorded on a large chart.

- In this book, the author quickly engages the readers as she asks them to imagine themselves being very small, hidden in a tiny egg. She takes them on an imaginative journey, experiencing the transformation from a caterpillar to a Black Swallowtail butterfly. Read the book to the children and later reread it. During a second reading, students can dramatize the text by acting out the stages of the developing insect. For further ideas on dramatizing the process of metamorphosis, see the **Dramatic Play** section.

- Ask students to observe how the author arranges the words on the page to create a poetic text. Discuss with the children how the word arrangement affects the way the text is read. This book provides a good model for students writing their own poetry about butterflies.

- Take time to examine and discuss the powerful illustrations by Lynne Cherry. They may inspire students to produce original artwork featuring butterflies and their nectar sources. Students can paint a flower garden with watercolors or tempera, adding bits of construction or tissue to create added dimensions. They can then draw and cut out a variety of butterflies and glue them onto the flowers in varying positions. The **Art** section (Butterflies) contains additional ideas for creating a butterfly garden mural.

Amazing Butterflies & Moths by John Still
ALL CONCEPTS

- This book is an excellent reference source for general information about butterflies and specific facts about various species. Read short sections aloud, showing students the vivid illustrations and sharing the interesting facts. Reading factual material aloud to students expands their knowledge, stimulates further learning, and builds familiarity with the structure of nonfiction literature.

- Students can write and illustrate their own books about butterflies. As they familiarize themselves with a variety of informational books, they will see examples of different charts, graphs, and illustrations. Discuss the effectiveness of these different visuals and encourage students to incorporate some of these formats in their own books.

The Lamb and the Butterfly by Arnold Sundgaard
SCIENCE CONCEPT 3: Basic Needs

- Read *The Lamb & the Butterfly*, a gentle, rhythmic story about two different ways of life. The beautiful illustrations are by Eric Carle.

- Encourage the children to discuss their reactions to the two main characters. Emphasize that there is no correct or incorrect response. A variety of reactions is wonderful. Ask students to summarize the author's message.

- The texture of the art in this text is particularly inviting. Students may wish to create finger paint and paper collages in response to the story.

The Butterfly Hunt by Yoshi
SCIENCE CONCEPT 3: Basic Needs

- Read *The Butterfly Hunt,* a story of a little boy who furiously chases and catches a butterfly, then realizes he should set it free to live its own life.

- Discuss the meaning of freedom and the implications of catching insects for "pets."

- Students may wish to write about an insect they caught or why they think butterflies should be free.

- Look at Yoshi's illustrations of butterflies. Discuss the soft, muted colors of the artwork and the variety of butterflies portrayed. These drawings may inspire children to experiment with the art technique used by Yoshi, painting on fabric.

NOTES

READERS THEATRE

- Readers Theatre scripts are often created from picture books. Texts with several characters, a good amount of dialog exchange, and a predictable structure are particularly appropriate for a script. Begin by reading the story in its picture book format (large or small) so that the children can see the pictures and become familiar with the language and story sequence.

- Together, talk about turning the story into a play. Identify the character roles. Discuss how the nondialog lines should be handled. Make decisions about which parts should be read by solo voices, by partners, or by a chorus.

- Write the Readers Theatre script on a chart, a transparency for the overhead projector, or on script sheets. You may present the script, or students may cowrite the script with you, or students may write the scripts themselves, in small groups or individually.

- Model the script by reading it aloud. Invite the class to join in on the chorus.

- Together, assign parts. Suggest that actors highlight their assigned lines on their script sheet with a marker.

- Tape record the students reading the script. Playing it back provides valuable reinforcement, and the participants will enjoy hearing themselves on tape.

The Very Hungry Caterpillar by Eric Carle
SCIENCE CONCEPTS 2 and 3: Metamorphosis; Basic Needs

- Refer to the Readers Theatre guidelines and create a Readers Theatre script with the students.

- You may want to designate one reader for each day of the week, or you can assign one reader to Monday, two readers to Tuesday, etc. A chorus can read, in unison, the refrain: *But he was still hungry.* One student or a series of students can read the rest of the narration.

- Students can make visuals (one apple, two pears, etc.) to hold up as the parts are read. These visuals will also provide cues for the readers.

- There are many other ways to extend students' involvement with this book. You may wish to refer to the suggestions in the Books portion of the **Language Arts** section and the **Dramatic Play** section.

What Will You Be?

SCIENCE CONCEPT 2: Metamorphosis

- This original script lends itself to a Readers Theatre performance. It can also be made into a predictable Big Book featuring the children's illustrations. Each page will give a clue to the next.

- These parts can be assigned for script reading:

| Mother | Egg | Chrysalis |
| Christopher King | Caterpillar | Butterfly |

What Will You Be?

Mother:	Christopher King, what will you be, What will you be when you grow up?
Christopher King:	I am me. This is me. This is how I will always be.
Christopher King:	Hello, little egg. What will you be? What will you be when you grow up?
Egg:	I expect I will be a caterpillar. I am me. This is me. But this is not how I will always be.
Christopher King:	Hello, little caterpillar. What will you be? What will you be when you grow up?
Caterpillar:	I expect I will be a chrysalis. I am me. This is me. But this is not how I will always be.
Christopher King:	Hello, little chrysalis. What will you be? What will you be when you grow up?
Chrysalis:	I expect I will be a butterfly. I am me. This is me. But this is not how I will always be.

Christopher King:	Hello, little butterfly. What will you be? What will you be when you grow up?
Butterfly:	I am me. This is me. This is the final stage for me. I'll leave behind some small round eggs. And a beautiful new life will start from me.

An Invitation to the Butterfly Ball by Jane Yolen

SCIENCE CONCEPT 2: Metamorphosis

- Read this wonderful cumulative tale a number of times so that children can become familiar with the language and the events.

- Then, divide the text into parts. Assign students to read the lines of the various animals:

one mouse	six owls
two moles	seven raccoons
three rabbits	eight foxes
four skunks	nine frogs
five turtles	ten porcupines

Everyone can read the refrain in unison: *Knock, knock. Who's come to call!/ An invitation to the Butterfly Ball.*

I Wish I Could Fly
SCIENCE CONCEPT 2: Metamorphosis

- Children can read this Readers Theatre script, then later create and perform their own innovated versions, inserting new characters and locations.

- Together, decide who will be responsible for these roles:

Caterpillar	Reader 3	Narrator
Reader 1	Reader 4	
Reader 2	Reader 5	

I Wish I Could Fly

Reader 1: In the meadow, the caterpillar saw a bird.
The caterpillar said,

Caterpillar: Oh, how I wish I could fly!

Reader 2: In the garden, the caterpillar saw a dragonfly.
The caterpillar said,

Caterpillar: Oh, how I wish I could fly!

Reader 3: In the park, the caterpillar saw a beetle.
The caterpillar said,

Caterpillar: Oh, how I wish I could fly!

Reader 4: In the forest, the caterpillar saw a bee.
The caterpillar said,

Caterpillar: Oh, how I wish I could fly!

Reader 5: In the marsh, the caterpillar
saw a mosquito. The caterpillar said,

Caterpillar: Oh, how I wish I could fly!

Narrator: The caterpillar ate and ate,
then rested and rested. Soon
he became a chrysalis, and
later emerged as a butterfly.

Caterpillar (now a butterfly): I'm a butterfly! Oh, how I love to fly!

The Very Busy Butterfly

SCIENCE CONCEPTS 2 and 3: Metamorphosis; Basic Needs

- A Readers Theatre Script entitled *The Very Busy Butterfly* can be created, based on Eric Carle's predictable book, *The Very Busy Spider.*

- Begin by reading the original book, *The Very Busy Spider,* several times. Encourage students to join in on the rereadings of the story, particularly with the chorus line: *But the spider didn't answer. She was very busy spinning a web.*

- Introduce the idea of creating an innovation of the book entitled, *The Very Busy Butterfly.* First have students determine what the butterfly is busy doing: sipping nectar, laying eggs, drying his/her wings, etc. This will become the story refrain, to be read by the chorus: *The butterfly didn't answer. She was very busy (laying an egg). Off she flew to another (milkweed).*

- Let students brainstorm a group of animals that could converse with the busy butterfly. Write their suggestions on a chart. You may want to encourage students to choose animals that are likely to be found in butterfly habitats. One class selected these characters for their innovated Readers Theatre script:

cow	cricket	cat
wren	pig	goose
dog	hen	child

- Decide who will play which role. An individual, a small group of students, or the entire class can be assigned to the role of narrator.

- If students wish, they can enhance the performance by creating simple costumes (a tail, ears, nose) and small props.

- As an alternative to a Readers Theatre script, this innovated text can be developed into a predictable Big Book that students can illustrate.

NOTES

WRITING EXPERIENCES

Writing provides students with an opportunity to clarify their understandings, reflect on their learning, and share their ideas. A variety of writing experiences have been suggested throughout the Science and Social Studies sections. Some of these suggestions are elaborated in this section. Other writing ideas are presented as well.

LANGUAGE ARTS

We feel students should engage in a wide variety of writing situations. They should be encouraged to write for different purposes, write to different audiences, and experiment with different literary genres. The Writing Experiences in this section have been divided into six categories. We hope you and your students explore experiences from all six areas.

Labels, Lists, Charts, and Webs
Journals, Learning Logs, and Observation Sheets
Poetry
Books
Reports
Letters

Labels, Lists, Charts, and Webs

- Students can label or write about their drawings, diagrams, paintings, constructions, etc.

- Students can create signs for displays, bulletin boards, or the dramatic play area.

- Students can use their own spelling, or the teacher can take dictation for the children, depending on what is appropriate for the children and the experience.

- As students read or listen to information, consider creating lists, webs, or charts to record and organize information for discussion or reference. Children or the teacher can list vocabulary or phrases on charts as they are discussed.

- Throughout the **Science** and **Social Studies** sections are suggestions for teacher and students to brainstorm ideas, record and organize information, and share ideas through the use of charts and webs.

- Whenever possible, develop these charts and webs cooperatively. Encourage students to contribute the parts they can: sentences, words, or sounds. This becomes a "shared" writing experience, with both teacher and students creating the text.

- As the students brainstorm or make charts, help them organize thoughts and determine categories. Ask questions such as the following:

  Where should we put this idea or question?
  Can we give this group of ideas a name?
  How should we word that idea?
  Would anyone like to write that part?
  How should we start to write "metamorphosis?
  What should we write at the end?

- When they have seen many demonstrations and participated often in this type of group writing, students will be able and motivated to use the skills independently, recording and organizing information into charts, webs, and outlines.

NOTES

Journals, Learning Logs and Observation Sheets

ALL CONCEPTS

- Journals and Learning Logs provide excellent tools for recording observations, new understandings, questions, or reflections. For convenience, you may want to keep copies of the reproducible Observation Sheet provided in Appendix A near the cage of the classroom butterfly. Students can draw and write as they observe. The dated Observation Sheets can later be bound together into an Observation Book.

- Student entries in the journals and learning logs can vary in content and focus. You may want to brainstorm different possibilities with the students. They can include:

  - observations or labelled drawings of the classroom butterfly at different stages
  - personal thoughts, original poetry
  - fictional or true stories related to butterfly experiences
  - responses to books or stories, field trips, or visiting speakers
  - new questions or insights
  - data gathered from observation, reading, or field trips
  - favorite poems, copied and illustrated

NOTES

Poetry

ALL CONCEPTS

- In this section we have included suggestions for writing concrete poems, haiku, acrostic poems, "innovated" verses following the pattern of published poetry, limericks, tongue twisters, and free verse. This selection is meant to stimulate experimentation with the many ways students can share their ideas in poetic form.

CONCRETE POEMS

- Concrete poems are words shaped into the form of the subject itself. A poem about a butterfly can be written to form the shape of a butterfly; a poem about a caterpillar can form its shape.

Students can observe a caterpillar or a butterfly and write a poem in its shape.

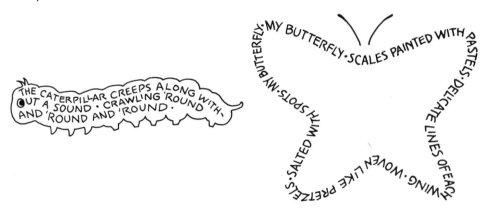

HAIKU

- Haiku is a form of Japanese poetry. It is usually about nature and consists of a few lines based on a syllable count. Using a three-line form with five syllables, seven syllables and five syllables, demonstrate the writing of several pieces, such as the one below.

  Monarch butterfly
  Twirling, dancing gracefully
  Blazing gem, dart by

- Individually, in groups, or as partners, have students compose haiku of their own. Their verses can be illustrated with black pen and watercolor paintings, then collated into a class book.

ACROSTIC POEMS

- An acrostic poem is a poem designed with the name of the object written vertically down the left side. Each letter on a line is used to begin a word, phrase, or sentence about the poem subject. The word "butterfly" or the names of the various butterflies can be used to write an acrostic poem.

>   Beautiful
>   Unusual
>   Twirling
>   Tender
>   Elegant
>   Rare
>   Fluttering
>   Lovely
>   Yellow

INNOVATED POEMS

- An innovated poem is a variation based on an existing poem with a predictable structure. After reading the existing poem several times, students can insert their own words to create a new piece.

- Innovated poems based on "Fragile Butterfly." The following poem, "Fragile Butterfly," can be written in large print on chart paper and used for Shared Reading. When students know the poem well, they can compose a poem of their own, using the same basic structure but inserting the names of other butterfly food sources. They may also choose to substitute the name of a specific species for the word "butterfly" and/or select a different adjective to replace "fragile." Students can draw or paint each flower mentioned in the innovated poem and use the illustrations to decorate a poem poster or each page in a class Big Book.

Fragile Butterfly

Fragile butterfly

> sip from the Queen Anne's lace
> sip from the Black-Eyed Susan
> sip from the coreopsis
> sip from the milkweed

Then lay your eggs.

- Innovated poems based on "Mice" by Rose Fyleman. Write the poem "Mice" by Rose Fyleman in large print on chart paper. The poem can be found in a number of anthologies including *Read-Aloud Rhymes for the Very Young, Sing a Song of Popcorn,* and *The Random House Book of Poetry.* (See the Bibliography for complete references.)

  Enjoy the poem a number of times through Shared Reading. Discuss the poem pattern. Then, with the students, innovate a poem about butterflies, using the structure of the "Mice" poem. You may want to write a "framework" for the innovated poem on a transparency or a chart, deleting the words from "Mice" that are specifically about mice and providing blank lines for innovated phrases:

  I think _____ are _____ .

  Students do not have to reproduce the rhyme schemes Rose Fyleman used in "Mice;" the poem should simply serve as a springboard and a supportive pattern.

  After composing a number of group poems, encourage individuals and partners to create their own innovated verses. Students may enjoy writing poems about a particular butterfly species they have studied. Students can create artwork to accompany their innovated verses.

- Innovated poems based on "Giraffe" by Mary Ann Hoberman. Write the poem "Giraffe" by Mary Ann Hoberman in large print on chart paper. The poem can be found in *Eric Carle's Animals Animals.*

  Enjoy the poem "Giraffe" a number of times through Shared Reading. Discuss the poem pattern. Then, with the students, innovate a poem about butterflies, using the structure of the "Giraffe" poem. You may want to start your innovated poem with the lines:

  We like them.
  Ask us why.
  Because _____ .

  You may want to write a "framework" for the innovated poem on a transparency or a chart, deleting the words from "Giraffe" that are specifically about giraffes and providing blank lines for innovated phrases.

  After composing a number of group poems, encourage individuals and partners to create and illustrate their own innovated verses about butterflies. The poems can be bound together in a class book entitled *We Like Butterflies.*

- Innovated poems based on "Children, Children Everywhere" by Jack Prelutsky. Write the poem "Children, Children Everywhere" by Jack Prelutsky on a transparency or in large print on chart paper. The poem can be found in *The Random House Book of Poetry for Children.*

Read the poem aloud a number of times. Invite the students to join in, reading in unison or assigning pairs of lines to individuals or partners.

Then, using the basic structure of Prelutsky's poem, innovate a new poem with the students, "Caterpillars, Caterpillars Everywhere." Write verses describing caterpillars, their behavior, and their variety. After completing the group poem, some students may be interested in innovating their own poems about caterpillars or butterflies, others may be interested in publishing the class poem in book form, copying one or two lines of the poem on each page and adding illustrations.

- Many other poems and chants lend themselves to innovations. New verses can easily be created for the songs in the **Music** section. Students can write innovations with teacher guidance, in cooperative peer groups, or individually.

LIMERICKS

- Gather a collections of limericks and share several limericks with the students each day to model the form for students. Edward Lear's limericks are famous and a great deal of fun.

- Ask students what they notice all limericks have in common. They should note the five lines, the rhythm, and the rhyming pattern: lines 1, 2, and 5 rhyme and lines 3 and 4 rhyme. Usually limericks are humorous, and often the final line is a repeat or a near repeat of the opening line.

- Students can start out by writing a limerick using their own name: *There was a young lady called Kerry. . .* or *There was a young fellow named Carlos. . .*

- Try writing caterpillar or butterfly limericks cooperatively, as a class. Here is an example:

   There was a caterpillar from Lynn
   Who was very hairy and thin
   One day she strayed
   To sip some lemonade
   But it all ended when she fell in.

- Students can write their own caterpillar or butterfly limericks, working individually or in pairs.

- Compile a class book of limericks accompanied by humorous illustrations.

TONGUE TWISTERS

- Tongue Twisters are sentences in which most of the words begin with or include the same sound. Together, compose a few butterfly or caterpillar tongue twisters. Here are some examples. Try to say each one fast, three times in a row.

  Beautiful butterflies breezed by bunches of begonias.
  Crowds of creeping caterpillars crawled carefully.

- Working individually or with a partner, students can write and illustrate tongue twisters. Display the class work and try reading the tongue twisters together . . . fast!

FREE VERSE

- Read a wide variety of rhyming and free verse poetry to students so that they will realize that poetry is a special way of knowing and expressing ideas. It doesn't always rhyme. The Poetry section in the Bibliography recommends a diverse selection of butterfly-related poems. They are referenced throughout the **Science** and **Social Studies** sections.

- As students expand their knowledge and understanding of butterflies, they will communicate their thoughts in many ways. Invite them to express their ideas by drawing or painting, and by writing free verse.

- Set aside time for reading student poetry aloud. Prepare a display with poetry and accompanying artwork.

NOTES

Books

- A thematic study rich in information lends itself to the creation of large or small published books as a means of sharing and summarizing one's learning. Books can be written by individuals, groups, or the class.

- Any favorite story, poem, or song can be enlarged, paired with children's art, and compiled into a Big Book to provide interesting, familiar, and enjoyable reading material.

- Caterpillar-shaped, butterfly-shaped, or rectangular books of all sizes can be published to celebrate and share stories or new learning. They can use the same pattern of a book read by the class, incorporating new words or adding further adventures. These can be class, group, or individual books.

- Students may wish to create a large informational book about butterflies for others to read.

- Class books of butterfly riddles, poetry, legends, or information can provide more reading material for all students.

A BUTTERFLY A DAY BIG BOOK
SCIENCE CONCEPT 5: Variety

- Each day, the class can select and learn about a different butterfly or family of butterflies. After reading, listening, and discussing the butterfly, have students compose a few sentences about it. Write the sentences on a large piece of chart paper or thin poster board. Leave plenty of space around the text.

- Students can draw, paint, or make collage pictures of the featured butterfly, then glue the pictures on the chart. Punch holes, add rings and a cover, and these charts can easily become a Big Book for all to read.

ABC BOOKS AND WALL POSTERS

SCIENCE CONCEPT 5: Variety

- Alphabet books offer students a wonderful avenue for writing and drawing about their new understandings. Display and discuss a variety of alphabet books so students can see possible formats. One good example is *The Icky Bug Alphabet Book* by Jerry Pallotta.

- Create a class alphabet book of various butterflies, or have each student create his or her own alphabet book. On each page have students write: the alphabet letter in large print, the complete butterfly name, and some information about the butterfly. A drawing of the butterfly completes the page.

- For the class alphabet book, use large pages. Each letter page can be done by a different child. Students can use a variety of art materials to add texture to their butterfly illustrations.

- The class *Butterfly ABC Big Book* can be taken apart to form a set of alphabet wall posters.

- Make field guides and other butterfly books available for the students to use as reference. The following list identifies a species the students may investigate for each letter; but there are many other options students will find themselves.

A	American Copper	N	Nevada Fritillary
B	Blues	O	Orange Tips
C	Cabbage White	P	Painted Lady
D	Duskywings	Q	Queen
E	Emperor	R	Ringlets, Red Admiral
F	Fritillaries	S	Skippers
G	Goatweed	T	Tortoise Shell
H	Hackberry	U	Uncas Skipper
I	India Skipper	V	Viceroy
J	Julia	W	Wood Nymphs
K	Kallima Inachus (Latin name)	X	Xami Hairstreak
L	Leafwings	Y	Yellows
M	Monarch	Z	Zebra Swallowtail

Aa is for Admiral
The Red Admiral is a butterfly that lives in the woods, on farms and in backyards across the USA.

It likes the nectar of the butterfly bush.
It also likes fruit.
The larva likes the leaves of nettles and hops.

WE LIKE CATERPILLARS BIG BOOK
SCIENCE CONCEPT 5: Variety

- Provide the students with a variety of art materials such as crayons, chalk, oil pastels, construction paper, tissue paper, and other recycled material.

- After discussing and looking at drawings or photographs of a variety of caterpillars, have each student make a caterpillar using the various materials.

- As a group, look at the children's caterpillar drawings, and develop a list of words to describe them. Write these words on large chart paper.

- Together, create the text for a Big Book utilizing the drawings and the words from the list. The following is an example created by a group of students:

page 1	There are all kinds of caterpillars
page 2	large caterpillars
page 3	small caterpillars
page 4	fat caterpillars
page 5	skinny caterpillars
page 6	striped caterpillars
page 7	spotted caterpillars
page 8	smooth caterpillars
page 9	furry caterpillars
page 10	We like caterpillars. Do you?

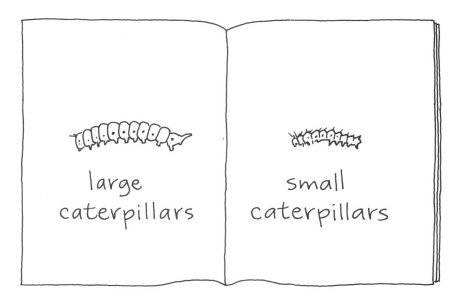

- The book can be expanded with the same kind of text and illustrations created with phrases: *caterpillars on tree trunks, caterpillars on grass, etc.*

- A *We Like Butterflies* Big Book can be created through the same process.

LIFE CYCLE STORY
SCIENCE CONCEPTS 2 and 5: Metamorphosis; Variety

- Read aloud a variety of books about the life cycle of the butterfly. Refer to the books recommended in the **Science** section (Concept 2: Metamorphosis).

- Have each student choose a butterfly, and create a book illustrating and writing about its metamorphosis from egg to butterfly. A book can be made from a series of pages containing a space for the illustrations and lines for the text. Another possible format is an accordion book. Students will probably have many other ideas: pop-up books, flap books, etc. Encourage students to find and share books that use unusual formats, and let them explore different ways of presenting information in their own books.

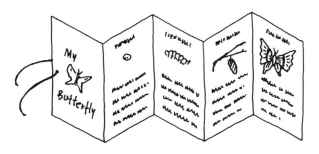 

NOTES

Reports

As students pose questions and solve problems, they need guidance in developing an understanding of the variety of ways they can share the information. Below, we have outlined a possible process for fostering the development of report-writing skills.

BUTTERFLY REPORT
ALL CONCEPTS

- Read a book about a particular butterfly. See the Bibliography for suggestions. You may wish to begin with a book about the species developing in the classroom.

- After reading the book or a few books, ask the students to recall and brainstorm information. Enlist their help in developing categories for their information. Together, create an informational web.

Habitat — Monarch
Meadows, roadsides, wherever milkweed is found

Range —
All of United States

How It Overwinters —
Migrates to Mexico
Stage - Butterfly

Special Information —
People tag monarchs to learn about their migration

Appearance
Egg - pale yellow/white
Caterpillar - white, yellow and black bands around body
Chrysalis - pale green with gold dots; turns dark before hatching
Butterfly - orange wings with black trim and white dots at edges
Wing span - 3½-4"

Food Preferences
Caterpillar - only milkweed
Butterfly - variety of nectar sources

- Once a model web has been constructed, have students pose questions to ask about other butterfly species. Create a chart form of their questions as a model for organizing information on other butterflies. There can be a space for answers and a space to record how or where the children found the information.

Reporters:		
Butterfly:		
Question	Answer	How We Found Out
What do the different stages look like?		
How big is the butterfly?		
What does it eat? larva: butterfly:		
Where does it live?		
What kind of habitat does it like?		
How does it spend the winter?		
Is there anything else we should know?		

- Students can form partners or groups to research a specific butterfly. To select an interesting species, they may wish to look through butterfly books and guides.

- Have partners or groups read, brainstorm, categorize, and chart their information to present to the class.

- As they learn about their butterfly's wingspan, how it overwinters or how it is classified by taxonomists, students can add this new information to the appropriate class chart or graph. For more details about these class charts and graphs, see the **Math** section for information on wingspan graphs, the **Science** section (Concept 3: Basic Needs) for information on overwintering charts, and the **Science** section (Concept 5: Variety) for information on butterfly classification charts.

- Students may wish to create visual material to communicate information, such as a drawing of the stages of the butterfly, a map of where the butterfly lives, or a poster of the preferred food.

- The final reports can be displayed for all to view. The reports can take a variety of forms: books, posters, charts, paintings, constructions.

Letters

ALL CONCEPTS

- During the butterfly theme study, there will be many purposeful opportunities for letter writing. Students can write letters or notes to:

  - order classroom butterflies or other related materials
  - request visits from entomologists, nature center personnel, or authors
  - arrange for a class field trip
  - request information from a scientist or a nature society
  - express environmental concern pertaining to butterfly habitats
  - invite parents to a class event
  - thank a classroom visitor or a field trip guide for his or her help

---

Mrs. Flynn's Class
Meadow School
322 Arthur St.
Concord, NY 12378

May 12, 1992

Concord Conservation Dept.
Town Office Building
235 Main St.
Concord, NY 12378

Dear Conservation Department,

Our first grade class is studying butterflies. We want to find out what our town is doing to help conserve or create habitats for butterflies and other animals.

We would like to have someone from your department come and talk to us and answer some of our questions.

We are in school from 8:45 to 3:00. Our telephone number is 842-0988. We look forward to hearing from you.

Sincerely,
Mrs. Flynn's Class

NOTES

MATH

The experiences in this section encourage children to use mathematical processes to advance their understandings about butterflies. Students are given a variety of opportunities to gather accurate data, organize bodies of information, and use the information to answer questions. The math experiences in this section flow naturally from the children's involvement in the theme study. Many, but certainly not all, important math concepts are explored.

The math experiences are divided into six categories:

Counting and Estimating
Graphing
Sequencing
Classifying
Exploring Symmetry
Computer Science

Through these experiences, students practice the following math processes:

describing	classifying	predicting
comparing	representing	generalizing
ordering	estimating	exploring

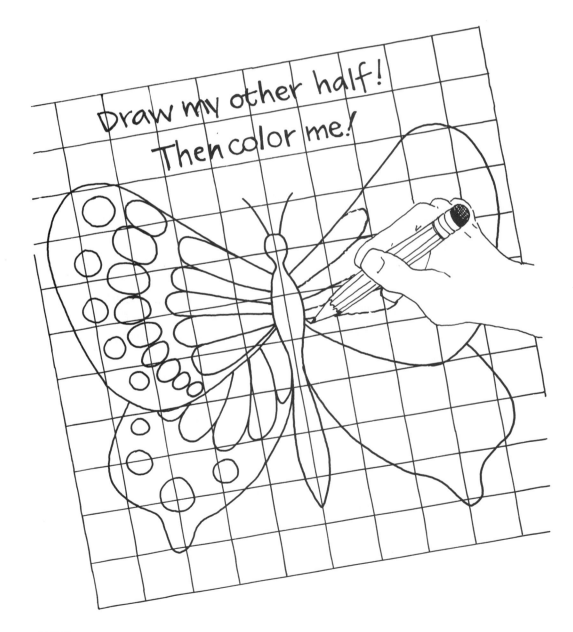

Draw my other half!
Then color me!

COUNTING AND ESTIMATING

Background Information

Scientists count butterflies in order to have a clear idea of how many butterflies exist within a given area. They compare data collected from one year to the next in order to monitor butterfly populations. It is not possible to count every butterfly in a given area, so scientists make estimates. Lepidopterists have developed four basic ways to estimate butterfly populations:

1. For part of one day, count every butterfly seen in a defined habitat. This method is used in the Fourth of July Counts. More information about the Fourth of July Count is provided below.

2. Count every butterfly seen along a specific path and within a set distance from the path. Usually one person repeats this count once a week, walking a standard path. The data is gathered from a variety of "walks" and the numbers are compared from year to year to determine the abundance of the species seen. These are referred to as Pollard Walks.

3. Count every butterfly in a specific area and then extrapolate a total number for a larger area in which the butterfly population should be the same. This method is used to estimate the number of overwintering monarchs in Mexico and California.

4. Compare the number of butterflies captured, marked, and released with the number of marked butterflies recaptured. This ratio can be used to estimate the number of butterflies in the total population. This approach is called the Mark-Release-Capture Method.

Counting butterflies can involve basic math skills or very sophisticated skills depending on the method used. For more detailed information on counting butterflies refer to the chapter, "Counting Butterflies" in Robert Pyle's, *The Audubon Society Handbook for Butterfly Watchers*.

If students want more information about the Fourth of July Butterfly Count they can contact:

> Xerces Society
> 10 Southwest Ash Street
> Portland, OR 97204

This count is usually done from mid-June through late July, but in some areas it is done as early as May. If students are interested in participating in the Fourth of July Butterfly Count, this might be a good time to enlist the help of a lepidopterist or a knowledgeable butterfly enthusiast. At least one person on the Butterfly Count must be able to identify butterflies. There are rules to follow, forms to fill out, and a slight charge to defray the cost of the survey.

Experiences

BUTTERFLY COUNT

SCIENCE CONCEPTS 3 and 5: Basic Needs; Variety

- Brainstorm and discuss reasons scientists might be interested in counting butterflies.

- Discuss different methods for counting and estimating butterfly populations. (Refer to the Background Information.)

- Choose a method or develop a way to count butterflies in a nearby habitat. The students will need to decide where, when, and how to count the butterflies as well as what to record and how to record the information gathered. Together, the class can develop a recording form. It might look something like this:

Name:	Susanne	
Butterfly Count		
Date: Sept. 18, 1992		
Weather: Sunny – 75°		
Place: Gray's Field		
Habitat: Meadow		
Size: 1 Acre+		
Time: 11:30 – 12:00		
Species	Number	
Monarch	|||	3
Common Sulphur	++++ |	6
Checkerspot	||	2
unknown	++++ ++++ ||	12

COUNTING POEMS AND CHANTS

SCIENCE CONCEPT 2: Metamorphosis

- Read the poems "This Little Caterpillar" and "Five Little Caterpillars," and the chant "Fly Away." The poems and the chant are provided in the **Language Arts** section.

- Read the poem "Ten Little Caterpillars" by Bill Martin, Jr. It is included in *Bill Martin Jr.'s Treasury Chest of Poetry*. See the Bibliography for more information.

BUTTERFLY BOARD GAME

SCIENCE CONCEPTS 2 and 3: Metamorphosis; Basic Needs

MATH

- Have the children design a board game that takes a butterfly through its life cycle and its encounters with nature and man. Use a spinner with numbers or number cubes for movement. Place blank stickers or draw squares on a rectangular or butterfly-shaped poster board to make a path. Complicate the movement with positive and negative events that occur during a butterfly's life cycle. If players land on a positive event, they can be instructed to move ahead extra spaces, get two turns, or take a shortcut. If they land on a negative event, players can move back two spaces, miss a turn, or take a long detour. Have a brainstorming session to develop ideas. Some possible events include:

Life Cycle
- egg hatches
- caterpillar molts
- caterpillar forms chrysalis
- butterfly hatches

Positive
- caterpillar finds lots of food
- chrysalis is well camouflaged
- drought ends with gentle rain
- flowers blossom

Negative
- birds feed young with larva
- food source cut down
- field sprayed with insecticide
- birds attack butterflies

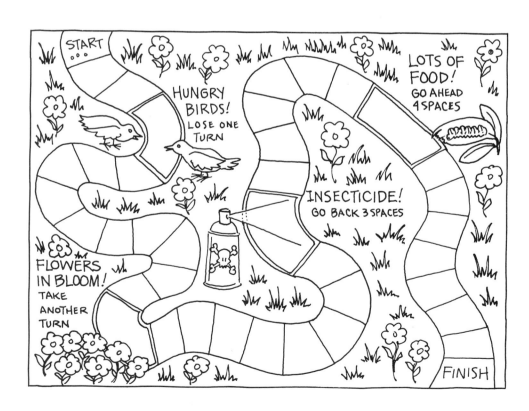

GRAPHING

LIFE CYCLE GRAPH

SCIENCE CONCEPT 2: Metamorphosis

- As a class, make a large graph recording the length of time the class butterfly spends in each stage of its life cycle. You will probably wish to graph only the stages the children observe. If observed, record the molts of the caterpillar on your graph. A Life Cycle Graph can be made in many different ways: using graph paper, paper squares (a different color for each stage of the life cycle), children's drawings, tally marks, or a calendar. Use the completed graph to discuss and compare the length of the different life stages.

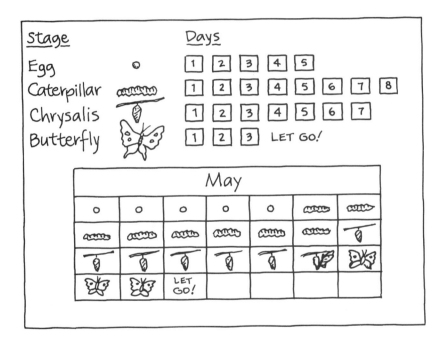

LIFE CYCLE TIME LINES AND TIME WHEELS

SCIENCE CONCEPT 5: Variety

- Make time lines or time wheels charting the length of each stage of development for different species. Divide the time lines or time wheels into the appropriate number of time segments (days, weeks, or months). Use a different color to chart the time spent in each stage of development. By reading each other's time lines, children can compare the length of time different butterflies spend in each life stage. Time wheels (like pie charts) can also be used to compare the amount of time different butterflies spend in each stage.

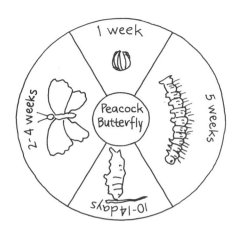

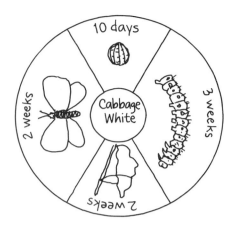

EATING GRAPH

SCIENCE CONCEPT 3: Basic Needs

- Chart the amount the class caterpillar eats each day. Compare the amount the caterpillar eats when it first hatches to how much it eats when it is older.

Wed.	Thurs.	Fri.	Sat. & Sun.	Mon.	Tues.	Wed.
Part of a leaf	Part of a leaf	Rest of leaf Plus ½	1½	2	0 (molted)	3

CATERPILLAR GROWTH GRAPH

SCIENCE CONCEPT 2: Metamorphosis

- Graph the length of the caterpillar. Because of the tiny size of a caterpillar, the small increments in growth, and age of the children, use concrete materials such as strips of paper or small objects to measure the caterpillar's length.

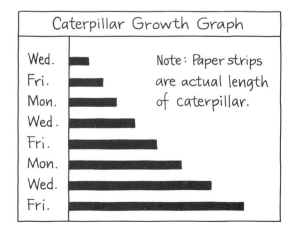

WINGSPAN GRAPHS

SCIENCE CONCEPTS 2 and 5: Metamorphosis; Variety

- Measure and graph the wingspan of the class butterfly. Compare it with the wingspans of the world's largest and smallest known butterflies. The largest butterfly (Queen Alexandra's Birdwing) has a wingspan of 8–9 inches if male, or up to 12 inches if female. The smallest butterfly (Western Pygmy Blue) has a wingspan of 0.4 inch.

- Use a large sheet of one-inch graph paper to record the wingspan of different butterfly species. Write the name of the butterfly and represent its wingspan by filling in the appropriate number of squares, one square to an inch. Students can find information about wingspans in butterfly guides. If children are writing reports on different butterflies, they can enter the wingspan of their butterfly on a class chart.

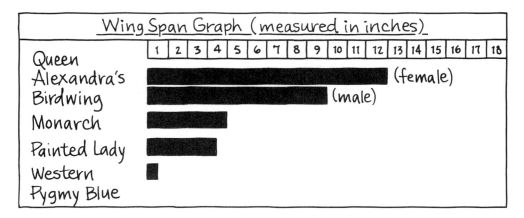

- With the children, make wingspan cards for a variety of butterflies. On a piece of paper, place a picture of a butterfly, write its name, and record its wingspan. The wingspan can be first written numerically and then shown with a measured line or a measured strip of colored paper. Have the children put the wingspan cards in order, from the smallest to the largest butterfly.

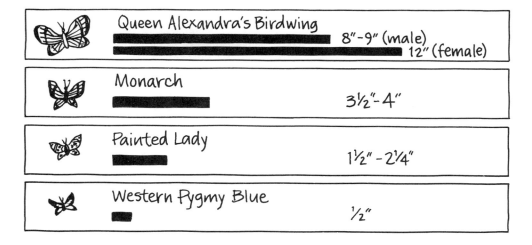

SEQUENCING

SEQUENCE PICTURES OF THE LIFE CYCLE

SCIENCE CONCEPT 2: Metamorphosis

- Have students draw the stages of the butterfly's life cycle and sequence them. See the **Art** section (Life Cycle) for ideas.

- Use the reproducible life cycle pictures provided in Appendix A for a sequencing activity.

- Purchase or make butterfly puzzles that involve sequencing the stages of the butterfly's life.

- Write a story, poem, or play about the butterfly's life cycle. See the **Language Arts** section for ideas (Writing Experiences: Books).

- Share finger plays, poems, and chants with a metamorphosis theme. There are many provided in the **Language Arts** section.

PATTERNING

SCIENCE CONCEPTS 2 and 5: Metamorphosis; Variety

- Have the students look at the class caterpillar or at pictures of caterpillars that have patterns, such as the Eastern Black Swallowtail caterpillar which has alternating plain black stripes and black stripes with yellow dots. Have the children describe the patterns of the different caterpillars. Then, let the children create model caterpillars with real or imaginary color patterns. Children can use pattern blocks, inch cubes, beads, or other manipulatives, or they can paint, use clay or stamps, or make collages with found objects. See the **Art** section (Caterpillars) for further ideas.

MATH

CLASSIFYING

MATCHING GAMES

SCIENCE CONCEPT 5: Variety

- Make and play matching games that require students to observe carefully: dominoes, Concentration (Memory), Lotto, etc. Students can match identical butterflies, caterpillars, or chrysalises, or they can match the corresponding caterpillars and adult butterflies. Matching games can be made from posterboard and pictures cut or photocopied from books, wrapping paper, stickers, etc. Two good sources for pictures are the photographs in the *Audubon Society Pocket Guide: Familiar Butterflies* and Carol Belanger Grafton's set of 87 authentically detailed drawings found in *Butterfly Stickers in Full Color.* Both can be purchased from Papillon Distributors, Inc. See the Bibliography and Appendix C for more information.

CLASSIFICATION GAME

SCIENCE CONCEPT 5: Variety

- Make a copy of the butterfly outline pictures found in Appendix A. Cut along the straight lines to make a set of picture cards. Use the cards to help students sort and classify butterflies by their wing shape.

  Place a few butterfly cards in front of the children. Ask how the wings are the same and how they are different. Repeat the process with different butterfly cards. Gradually increase the number of cards and see if the children can find ways to group the butterflies according to different wing shape attributes.

EXPLORING SYMMETRY

SYMMETRY OBSERVATION

SCIENCE CONCEPT 2: Metamorphosis

- Look at the class butterfly and/or pictures of butterflies with their wings spread. Have the students discuss the patterns on the wings. Their comments may reveal an awareness of the concept of symmetry, but they may need to be introduced to the term. Encourage children to use the words *symmetrical* and *symmetry* as they describe the butterfly wing patterns.

SYMMETRY CARDS

SCIENCE CONCEPT 2: Metamorphosis

- Cut out pictures of butterflies, paste each one on a square of tagboard, and cut in half, lengthwise. Students can match one half of the butterfly to the other half.

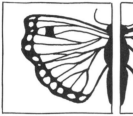   

- Provide students with a plastic mirror and a card showing one half of a butterfly. By holding the butterfly card against the mirror, they can create a whole butterfly and make it flap its wings.

 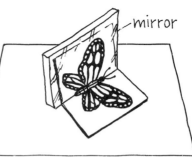

mirror

SYMMETRICAL ART

SCIENCE CONCEPT 2: Metamorphosis

- Have the students use graph paper and crayons, markers, or colored pencils to draw a symmetrical butterfly. The body of the butterfly should be placed in the center of the graph paper and the wings drawn on either side. Students can create symmetrical wing patterns of imaginary or known butterflies.

- Create a symmetrical painting or collage of a butterfly. See the **Art** section (Butterflies) for ideas.

COMPUTER SCIENCE

COMPUTER DRAWN BUTTERFLIES

SCIENCE CONCEPT 2: Metamorphosis

- Use a computer graphics program to draw any stage of the butterfly. If the program has a symmetry feature, children will be able to make a symmetrical butterfly easily. The children can add text to label their drawings or to write a story.

mi butrfli flu awa toda

NOTES

SOCIAL STUDIES

The experiences in this Social Studies section enable students to learn more about each other and their world while expanding their knowledge of butterflies. Following their particular interests, students can explore a wide range of topics. For example, they can read butterfly myths and legends from several countries, chart the route of migrating Monarchs on a map, or investigate the butterfly habitats found in their neighborhoods.

The experiences have been organized into four categories:

Butterfly History
Butterfly Geography (Science Concepts 3 and 5: Basic Needs, Variety)
Butterfly Conservation (Science Concepts 3 and 5: Basic Needs, Variety)
Butterfly Gardening (Science Concepts 3 and 5: Basic Needs, Variety)

Through these experiences, students will practice the processes used by social scientists:

sorting, organizing, and comparing information
classifying ideas
summarizing and presenting information
developing questions
exploring relationships
drawing and labelling diagrams
interpreting map information

BUTTERFLY HISTORY

Background Information

The first primitive moths lived about 140 million years ago. Butterflies appeared later. The oldest butterfly fossil discovered so far is about 40 million years old. The last dinosaurs died about 65 million years ago. Thus, butterflies and dinosaurs never coexisted. Homo sapiens (humans) have only existed for the last 100,000 years.

Experiences

- Discuss when butterflies first appeared on earth. Background information is provided in *Butterfly & Moth* by Paul Whalley (page 6).

- Find out what other animals were alive when the butterflies first appeared.

- Make a time line noting when certain animals first appeared on earth. Include familiar animals such as dinosaurs, sharks, cockroaches, moths, butterflies, horses, dogs, cats, spiders.

- Read stories that reveal what different groups of people have believed about butterflies:

  "How the Butterflies Came to Be" is a Papago tale found in *Keepers of the Animals: Native American Stories and Wildlife Activities for Children* by Michael J. Caduto and Joseph Bruchac.

  "How God Made the Butterflies" is an African-American story found in *Black Folktales* by Julius Lester.

- Read other legends and folktales about butterflies:

  "The Three Butterflies" found in *More Tales from the Welsh Hills* by Ellen Pugh.

  "The Spring Butterflies" found in *The Spring of Butterflies and Other Folktales of China's Minority Peoples* edited by Neil Philip.

- Research the origin of the word *butterfly*. Some information is offered in *The Butterfly Book* by Donald and Lillian Stokes and Ernest Williams.

SOCIAL STUDIES

BUTTERFLY GEOGRAPHY

Background Information

Butterflies live in all parts of the world except Antarctica. Most of the world's butterflies are found in the tropics. The South American rain forest has a particularly large and varied butterfly population. A few butterflies are seen north of the Arctic Circle.

Each species inhabits a precise geographical region. The size of such regions varies greatly; it may cover a few square miles of a mountain region or cover an entire continent. A few butterflies migrate, such as the Monarch. These species can be found in one location at one time of the year and in another location at another time. Butterfly guides contain information about the geographic range of individual butterflies.

Experiences

- Have children discuss the needs of butterflies (temperature, larval and adult food, etc.) and predict where in the world butterflies can and cannot survive. Look at worldwide distribution maps in butterfly field guides to confirm or disprove the children's predictions.

- If the class is studying different butterfly species, create a standard map and have the children shade the area of a map where a particular type of butterfly can be found. Have them compare maps to see if any of the butterflies being studied live in the same area or might be found in their town. If maps are created on acetate they can be compared by placing one on top of the other.

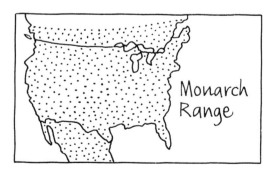 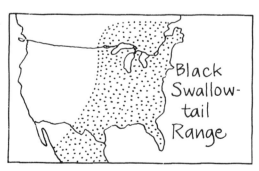

- Read about the habitats of different butterflies. Find out if butterflies can live in the desert, the tundra, the rain forest, the woods, etc.

- Use a globe or map to find the places where the Monarch butterfly migrates. The West Coast Monarchs fly to the Pacific Grove area, near Monterey in California. The East Coast Monarchs fly to the Cerro Pelon Mountains, west of Mexico City, Mexico.

BUTTERFLY CONSERVATION

Background Information

Particularly in the last 100 years, people have disturbed the life cycles of many butterfly species by destroying butterfly habitats and importing caterpillars and birds. In some cases this has led to the extinctions of a species. In other cases it has significantly lowered the butterfly population.

Butterfly habitats are destroyed by the construction of buildings, roads, and dams; they are destroyed when wetlands are drained, when roadsides are mowed, and when forests are cut down. Insecticides, fertilizers, and air and water pollution all contribute to the destruction of natural habitats.

Many species of butterfly are so closely linked to particular plants or groups of plants in a limited area that they are incapable of responding to the destruction of their habitat by flying elsewhere. The speed and extent of change do not allow them to evolve adaptations for survival and thus they become extinct.

The South American rain forest is the home of the largest butterfly population in the world. The deforestation of this area endangers a large number of butterfly species.

Butterflies form a valuable link in the food chain: they are a food source for many other animals. Butterflies are also valuable because they pollinate plants. When butterflies sip nectar from plants, pollen gathers on their body. As they move to the next plant, the pollen is transferred causing cross-pollination.

There are many things people can do to help ensure the survival of butterflies. They can protect and manage existing habitats, create new habitats and, on a large scale, raise and release butterflies. More specifically, people can:

- Educate the community on the beauty, habitats, needs, and perils of butterflies.

- Encourage organic gardening.

- Encourage planting species that are food for caterpillars and butterflies.

- Support organizations that promote butterfly conservation, such as the Xerces Society, or organizations that address more general environmental concerns, such as The Nature Conservancy, Audubon Society, Sierra Club, National Wildlife Federation, Wilderness Society, Friends of the Earth, and Defenders of Wildlife. The address for the Xerces Society is provided in Appendix D.

Experiences

- Discuss the effects human society has had on the life cycle of some butterflies. Ask, *What do the different stages of a butterfly need in order to live? What have people done that can cause these needs not be met?*

- Ask the students what actions they think can be taken to prevent widespread destruction of butterflies both locally and internationally. Encourage students to write to the Xerces Society and other conservation agencies for information about endangered butterfly species and ideas for ways students can help combat the situation. Addresses for several organizations are provided in Appendix D.

- Go on a butterfly walk. Look for butterflies and/or caterpillars and their food source. Notice what kind of habitat different butterflies prefer: woodlands, meadows, swamps, etc. Observe and discuss what is happening to the local habitats that could harm butterflies.

- Count the butterflies. For more information on counting butterflies see the **Math** section.

- Make a Butterfly Mural portraying local species of butterfly in a nearby habitat. See the **Art** section (Butterflies) for details.

- Find out what the children's town is doing to protect butterflies: setting aside conservation land, mowing roadsides in late summer rather than spring, etc.

- Find out what butterfly species in the local area (and in the world) are on the endangered list.

- Produce a "Butterfly Conservation Performance" for parents or other children in the school to help develop a deeper appreciation and concern for butterflies in today's world. This performance can be part of an event that marks the conclusion of the butterfly theme study. Students can create skits about what butterflies need to live, what kills butterflies, and the particular plants different caterpillars like to eat. They can include songs, poems, and chants from the **Language Arts** section. Refer to the **Dramatic Play** section for other presentation ideas.

- Read the poem "Hurt No Living Thing" by Christina Rossetti, found in the **Language Arts** section (Finger Plays, Poems, Chants).

BUTTERFLY GARDENING

Background Information

Butterfly gardening is a way to attract a wide variety of local butterflies to your flower garden. It is a way to increase habitats for butterflies on a small scale. The two basic requirements for a butterfly garden are: leaves for the caterpillars to eat, and flowers to entice and feed the butterflies. In general, the kinds of flowers that attract butterflies are bright, single flowers that provide a good place to perch and have a reachable nectar source. Some of the most common butterfly-attracting flowers include:

bee balm
phlox
zinnias
asters
lavender
larkspur
lobelia
nasturtium
pansies
cosmos
chives
Joe-Pye weed
viburnum
marigolds
sweet rocket
hyssop
dandelions
thistles
teasel
coralbells
baby's breath
primrose
yarrow
liatris

Queen Anne's Lace
Sweet William
coreopsis
black-eyed Susan
butterfly bush (buddleia)
butterfly weed
morning glory
candy tuff
lamb's ears
Veronica
mints
lantana
purple coneflower
ageratum
verbena
shasta daisy
sweet alyssum
lilac
heliotrope
goldenrod

Most caterpillars are "host specific" which means they will eat only one kind of plant, or plants belonging to one specific family. Below is a list of some of the well-known butterflies in the U.S. and the food source for the caterpillars (larvas).

Butterfly Name	Larval Food
Eastern Tiger Swallowtail	cherry, tulip trees, poplar, ash, birch, lilac
Western Tiger Swallowtail	willow, poplar, hops
Spicebush Swallowtail	spicebush, sassafras, sweet bay, prickly ash
Black Swallowtail	parsley, dill, wild carrot, parsnip, celery, Queen Anne's lace, anise
Anise Swallowtail	anise, sweet fennel, Queen Anne's lace
Red Admiral	nettles, hops
Spring Azure	viburnum, blueberries, dogwood, spirea, sumac, meadow sweet, cherry
Monarch	milkweed
Mourning Cloak	elm, willow, poplar, aspen, hackberry
Buckeye	plantain, gerardia, snapdragon, turtlehead
Viceroy	willows, poplars, aspen, apple, plum
Baltimore	turtlehead, plantain, penstemon, paintbrush
Hackberry	hackberry tree
Cabbage White	cabbage, broccoli, nasturtium, collards
American Painted Lady	everlasting, butterfly bush (buddleia)
Painted Lady	thistle, hollyhock, mallow
Pearl Crescent	asters
Regal Fritillary	violets

For more information on butterfly gardening, refer to:

The Butterfly Book by Donald and Lillian Stokes and Ernest Williams
Butterfly Gardening by Matthew Tekulsky
The Audubon Society Handbook for Butterfly Watchers by Robert Michael Pyle
"A Butterfly Garden" in *Theme Gardens* by Susan Damarosch
"Butterfly Gardening," a Xerces Society Self-Help Sheet by Jo Brewer

Experiences

- Discuss the idea and purpose of growing a butterfly garden.

- Examine and discuss the Smithsonian Institute poster "Butterflies and Their Flowers." Beautiful drawings show ten butterflies on their nectar sources:

  American Painted Lady on butterfly bush (buddleia)
  European Cabbage Butterfly on wild marjoram
  Gray Hairstreak on red clover
  Monarch on milkweed
  Orange Sulphur on butterfly weed
  Pearl Crescent on New England aster
  Pipe Vine Swallowtail on field thistle
  Silver Spotted Skipper on globe thistle
  Tiger Swallowtail on garden phlox
  Viceroy on Joe-Pye weed

  Ordering information for this poster is provided in the Bibliography.

- Children can find out what butterflies are found in their local area and what plants and flowers the caterpillars and butterflies need for food. Help them organize the information in lists and charts.

- Students can write about butterfly gardening, including a list of larval and butterfly food preferences, and make copies of the information to share with their families and neighbors. Local greenhouses or garden centers might be willing to distribute it to their customers or post the information with a display of some of the plants mentioned.

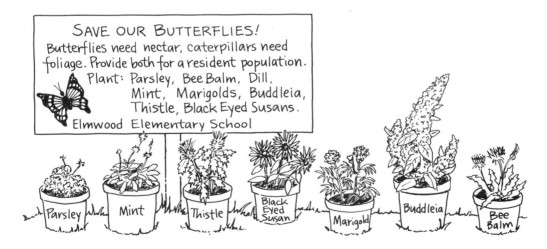

- If appropriate, the class can design and plant their own butterfly garden. If no garden plot is available on school grounds, a local garden center might be willing to donate space. Encourage students to put a sign on their butterfly garden explaining its purpose, and to label the plants.

SOCIAL
STUDIES

Butterfly Gardening   135

NOTES

ART

Art is a way of knowing, understanding, and expressing one's view of the world. It is an important form of communication for children. Through art they can express their ideas and emotions, as well as experiment with the possibilities offered by various art media. Often children use art to add to the meaning of their written work. The art experiences in this section enable children to participate in aesthetic experiences and help to further their understanding of butterflies.

Children should be encouraged to carefully observe the different stages of the class butterfly and to note and discuss the details that distinguish one type of butterfly from another. This attention to form, colors, textures, and patterns will help the children represent butterflies realistically or abstractly in their art.

For organizational purposes, the Art section has been divided into three categories:

Caterpillar Art Experiences
Butterfly Art Experiences
Life Cycle Art Experiences

CATERPILLAR ART EXPERIENCES

ALL CONCEPTS, especially 2 and 5: Metamorphosis; Variety

Caterpillar Observation

Before beginning a caterpillar art project, encourage the children to carefully observe the class caterpillar and to explore the resource guides that contain photographs and drawings of caterpillars. Discuss and chart the colors, patterns, coverings, special features, and size of the caterpillars observed in the guides.

Caterpillar Drawings and Paintings

After carefully observing the class caterpillar and looking at caterpillar pictures, draw or paint an actual or imaginary caterpillar. A variety of materials can be used: pencil, colored pencils, markers, crayons, oil pastels, chalk, watercolors, tempera, or any combination of the above, such as crayon and tempera, or marker and watercolors.

Clay Caterpillars

Use modeling clay to make caterpillar sculptures. If several colors are available, the color patterns can be represented. Realistic caterpillar sculptures can be encouraged by placing photographs and the Butterflies Abound Poster near the art area so children can use them as reference.

Egg Carton Caterpillars

Cut egg cartons in half lengthwise. If each section of the egg carton is used to represent a segment of the caterpillar, you may wish to staple or tape a few lengths together. Paint the egg carton caterpillar and let it dry. Later, create patterns, texture, and special feature by gluing on objects such as buttons, sequins, and pieces of paper. Form legs from paper, straws, pipe cleaners, sticks, etc. Students may wish to refer to the caterpillar diagram on the Butterflies Abound Poster to establish the proper placement of the legs. After the caterpillar is complete, it can be placed in a paper bag and hung on a branch to represent the chrysalis stage.

Recycled Caterpillars

Gather a variety of found and recycled round objects: bottle caps, buttons, pebbles, lids, sequins, plastic disks. Glue the objects on a piece of stiff paper to make a caterpillar. Add details and scenery with other media.

Fabric Caterpillars

Cut scraps of material into round pieces. The edges can be cut with pinking shears to give a hairy look, if desired. Children can glue the circles on a piece of stiff paper to make a fabric collage caterpillar. Smaller pieces of fabric, buttons, and trim can be glued on top for details.

Tissue Paper Caterpillars

Cut or tear tissue paper in "hot dog" shapes or circles. Arrange the caterpillar body parts on a piece of construction paper. Use a paintbrush to apply liquid starch (found in the laundry section of supermarkets) under and on top of the tissue paper. The liquid starch acts as a glue. It will be clear when it dries. As an alternative, use white liquid glue, watered down and applied with a paintbrush. Stripes and dots cut from tissue paper can be added as a second layer. When the tissue paper caterpillar is dry, additional details and scenery can be drawn or painted.

Stamp Printed Caterpillars

A stamp pad and a variety of stamps in geometric shapes can be used to create caterpillars. Children can use these stamps to create caterpillars with patterns. Details such as feet can be added when the ink is dry with pencil, markers, or crayons. Encourage children to describe the patterns that characterize their own caterpillars and the caterpillars their classmates have created.

Object Printed Caterpillars

Gather round objects such as corks and spools, or cut round shapes from potatoes or sponges. Use the round surfaces for printing the segments of a caterpillar. Dip the object into a pan of paint and press it on paper. The circles can be printed overlapping each other, or side by side. If several colors are available, color patterns can be created. When the body dries, details (such as legs and dots) and background can be added. If realism is desired, encourage the correct number of segments and leg placement.

Soft Sculpture Caterpillars

Stuff a sock or stocking with newspaper, material, fiberfill, styrofoam, etc. to form a caterpillar body. Close off the open end by sewing or by using a rubber band, a tie from garbage bag, or string. Decorate the caterpillar with material and objects that can be glued or sewn onto the body.

Pom-pom Caterpillars

Glue or sew pom-poms together. A giant class caterpillar or little individual caterpillars can be made. Paper dots, sequins, buttons, etc. can be glued on. The caterpillars can be freestanding or glued onto a piece of paper.

Cotton Ball Caterpillars

A caterpillar can be formed by gluing cotton balls together or by running a wire or a needle and thread through the center of each cotton ball. If a wire is used, bend both ends of the wire back to avoid sharp projections. Add details or decorations with glue.

NOTES

ART

BUTTERFLY ART EXPERIENCES

ALL CONCEPTS, especially 2 and 5: Metamorphosis; Variety

Butterfly Observation

Before beginning a butterfly art project, encourage the children to carefully observe the class butterfly and to explore the resource guides that contain photographs and drawings of butterflies. Discuss and chart the colors, patterns, special features, and size of the butterflies observed in the guides.

Butterfly Drawings and Paintings

After carefully observing butterflies, draw or paint an actual or imaginary butterfly, depending on the focus of the project. Choose from a variety of materials: pencil, colored pencils, markers, crayons, oil pastels, chalk, watercolors, tempera, or any combination of the above such as crayon and tempera, or marker and watercolors. Because butterflies have scales, glitter, sequins, or paper confetti might be appropriate materials to add to paintings and drawings.

Symmetrical Butterflies: Method 1.

To make a symmetrical painting of a butterfly, fold a piece of paper in half and then open it. On the fold, paint a line. To one side, paint the outline of the wings of the butterfly. The painting may look like the letter B. Add a painted antenna to that side. Then, paint or spatter tempera paint inside the B-shape. While the paint is wet, fold the sides together and press the surface with the palm of the hand. Open to let it dry.

Symmetrical Butterflies: Method 2.

Fold a piece of paper in half, then open it. Place paint the consistency of cream in squeeze bottles. Squeeze puddles of different color of paint onto one side of the paper. Close the paper and press sides together. Open and let dry. With the paper folded, draw half of a butterfly with the body on the folded edge. Cut the butterfly shape out.

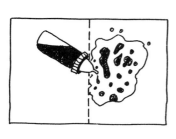 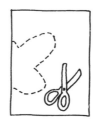  

Butterfly Murals

Paint a setting for butterflies (woodland, meadow, garden). When it is dry, add butterflies to the scene. Paint butterflies directly on the mural, or attach cut-out butterflies painted on separate pieces of paper. A 3-D effect can be created by attaching half of the butterfly to the mural and letting the other half flutter free. The butterflies can be fanciful and decorated with glitter and foil, or they can be realistic, modeled on specific species. The illustrations in Joanne Ryder's book, *Where Butterflies Grow*, may give students ideas and inspiration for their mural.

Giant Painted Butterfly

An overhead projector or opaque projector can be used to project an enlarged image of a butterfly on a piece of mural paper hanging on a wall. The students can trace and paint the butterfly.

Butterfly Sponge Painting

Cut pieces of paper into the shape of a butterfly, or draw the outline of a butterfly with a marker. Cut sponges into small pieces. Have students dip sponges into different colors of paint and dab paint on the butterfly shapes. To make it easier to handle the small pieces of sponge, clip them to spring-loaded clothesline pins. A styrofoam egg carton or ice tray can be used to hold the paint and the sponges when not in use. The more colors available, the more varied the butterflies will be.

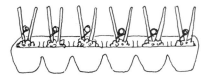

For a different butterfly art project, cut sponges in the shapes of different butterflies. Dip the sponges into pans of paint, and print. Children can create designs with many butterflies or with repeated prints of one butterfly. When dry, more details can be added with paint or other media.

Scratch Art Butterfly

Using many different colored crayons, completely cover a piece of stiff paper. Then paint over the crayon with black or dark blue paint. Using a stiff, rounded object such as a popsicle stick or nail head, draw a butterfly. As the paint is scraped away, different colors will emerge from beneath the paint.

Butterfly Stencil Rubbings

Cut cardboard, sandpaper, smooth or textured sheets of plastic into a variety of butterfly shapes. Place the butterfly shape under a piece of thin paper. Rub a crayon (remove the paper), a piece of chalk, or oil pastel over the surface of the paper. A butterfly shape will emerge. This process works best if the side of the drawing material, rather than the tip, is used. Place another butterfly under the paper and repeat the process. This can be done many times to create an overlapping design. If the paper moves during the rubbing process, the outline will not be clear. Students can tape the paper to the table to hold it in place.

Butterfly Finger Painting

Spread finger paint on a piece of finger-paint paper and draw a picture of a butterfly, using a finger. A print of this drawing can be made by placing a piece of construction paper over the finger painting, rubbing, and removing.

Butterfly Print

With a brayer, roll water-soluble printing ink on a table surface or a piece of plexi-glass. Using his or her fingertips, have a child draw a picture of a butterfly in the paint. Place a piece of paper on top of the drawing. Smooth the paper with the palm of the hand, then remove. You will have made a print of the drawing.

Styrofoam Printing

Cut off the edges of a styrofoam tray to make a flat printing surface. Using a pencil, draw a butterfly on the styrofoam. The lines should deeply etch the surface, but not go all the way through. Use a brayer to roll paint smoothly over the completed drawing. Place a piece of paper on top of the painted styrofoam surface, rub the paper with the palm of your hand, then peel the paper off the styrofoam. This printing process can be repeated many times. After looking at the first "artist proof" print, the artist can improve his or her work by making the lines of the drawing deeper, adding more details, etc. Try printing on colored paper and using different colors of ink. Multiple prints of the same drawing can be made on one piece of paper.

Stained Glass Butterflies

Make crayon shavings by scraping crayons with a vegetable peeler. Scatter the shavings on a piece of wax paper. When enough shavings have accumulated, cover with another piece of wax paper. Set an iron to the lowest setting. Iron until the shavings have melted and the two pieces of wax paper have fused. This activity takes only a few seconds. For safety, the iron should be handled by an adult, while the children help with the shavings and paper. The wax paper can either be cut out in the shape of a butterfly or it can be placed behind a frame of construction paper cut out in the shape of a butterfly. Place the "stained glass" butterflies in a window for dramatic viewing.

Butterfly Sculpture

Use modeling clay to create butterfly sculptures. Butterfly photographs and the diagram on the Butterflies Abound Poster may be used as references to encourage details. The children might want to place their butterfly on a flower base.

Symmetrical Butterfly Collage

Collect different types of paper: construction paper, wallpaper, gift wrap, tissue paper, etc. Select a large piece of paper and fold it in half. On the fold draw half of a butterfly. Cut out the butterfly. Decorate the butterfly with small duplicate shapes cut from two layers of another paper. In order to make the butterfly symmetrical, glue the duplicate shapes onto corresponding locations on each side of the butterfly. This art project can also be done with fabric.

Dip and Dye Butterflies

Provide paper coffee filters, or white or light-colored tissue paper cut into rectangles approximately 8 inches × 6 inches. Fold the filters or tissue paper rectangles several times to make smaller rectangles or triangles. Dip the corners or sides of the paper into different colors of food coloring. Repeat this process with another coffee filter or piece of tissue paper. Unfold the dyed papers and let them dry. Place the two papers in the slot of a clothespin and secure them with glue. The clothespin will serve as the body of the butterfly; the dyed paper will form the wings. Fluff the paper wings out. Add antennae and a proboscis, using pipe cleaners or paper. Add face features with markers.

Party Blower Butterfly

Use a commercial party blower as the head, thorax, and abdomen of a butterfly. The part of the blower that uncurls will be the butterfly's proboscis. Have the students cut out four symmetrical wings from paper (construction, wrapping paper, etc.) and glue them onto the stem of blower. Encourage a variety of wing shapes. Add six legs and antennae to make the butterfly as realistic as possible.

NOTES

LIFE CYCLE ART EXPERIENCES

SCIENCE CONCEPTS 2 and 5: Metamorphosis; Variety

Life Cycle Chart

Carefully observe and draw the classroom butterfly as it passes through each stage of its life cycle. If certain stages (egg and/or caterpillar) are not observed, find photographs of your butterfly species in these stages, and have students draw pictures using the photos as reference. When the classroom butterfly has emerged and the life cycle is complete, place each drawing on a large piece of paper. Label the drawings and add arrows to show the sequence of the cycle.

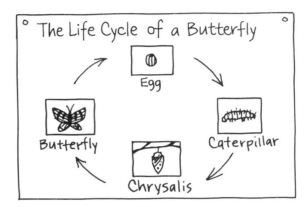

Life Cycle Puzzle

Trace a large circle on stiff paper. Draw jigsaw-like lines to divide the circle into four wedges. Have the children carefully observe and draw each stage of the life cycle, one in each section of the circle puzzle, in the order of occurrence. When the drawings are completed, have children cut the puzzle apart, along the jigsaw lines. A simpler circular puzzle could be made by cutting pie-shaped wedges from a circle with scissors or a paper cutter.

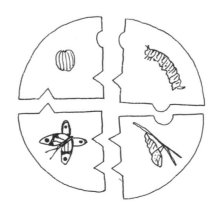

Life Cycle Spinner

Cut out two circles, one slightly larger than the other. Draw lines to divide the larger circle into quarters. Cut a pie wedge out of the edge of the smaller circle, removing approximately one fourth of the rim. The point of the wedge should not reach the center of the circle. (Refer to the drawing below.) Use a hole puncher to make a hole in the center of the smaller circle. Place the smaller circle on top of the larger circle. Use a brass fastener to attach the circles together through their centers. On the bottom circle draw the four stages of the life cycle, one in each quarter of the large circle. Each drawing should fit inside the wedge cut out of the top circle. Label the stages around the edge.

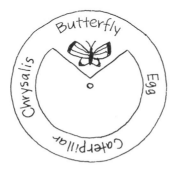

Life Cycle Mobile

Use a variety of art techniques to create 3-D representations of the four stages in a butterfly's life. Some possibilities are illustrated below. Make labels, then construct a life cycle mobile, using a wire coat hanger or a forked branch, string, a hole punch, and tape.

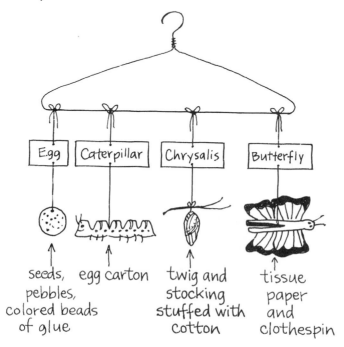

Finger Print Art

Press fingertips first on a stamp pad and then on paper. Use markers or crayons to add details and transform the ink finger prints into illustration of the four different stages in the butterfly's life cycle.

Life Cycle Puppets

Puppets enhance language arts and dramatic play experiences. Puppets representing the four stages of the butterfly life cycle can be made from a variety of materials.

- Finger puppets can be made from paper rings with pictures of characters glued on.
- Two-dimensional or three-dimensional characters can be attached to the fingertips of an old glove.
- Paper bags and old socks can be decorated and turned into hand puppets.
- Stick puppets can be made by cutting out drawings and gluing them to the ends of sticks.

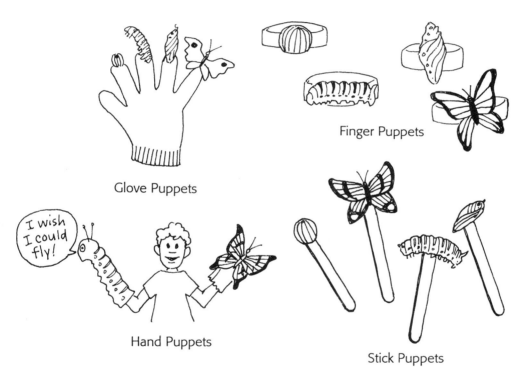

Glove Puppets

Finger Puppets

Hand Puppets

Stick Puppets

Life Cycle Costumes

Costumes can be made from material, large paper bags, and cardboard.

NOTES

DRAMATIC PLAY

Children gain new understandings as they engage in dramatic play experiences by assuming different roles: lepidopterist, museum guide, caterpillar, butterfly, etc. Many animated conversations will occur as children choose, plan, and execute their play. Given time, space, a few props, and teacher encouragement, dramatic play will flourish in many areas of the classroom. Such experiences can enrich children's understanding of all five science concepts.

Experiences

- Brainstorm ideas for transforming the dramatic play area into something related to butterflies. A butterfly habitat or a butterfly museum or store might be suggested. Once the idea is agreed upon, continue to brainstorm with the students in order to develop the theme. The brainstorm session might result in a chart like this:

	Butterfly Habitat	Butterfly Museum with Gift Shop
Props needed	trees, bushes, grass, flowers, all stages of a butterfly, birds, toads, binoculars, guide book, clipboard and paper for field notes	admission counter, tickets, sign, cash register, money, brochures, maps, shelves, display cases, labels for displays, goods to sell in gift shop
Things to make	scenery, animals, binoculars	butterflies for display, murals, price tags, things to sell (books, artwork, decorations), shelves and display cases (big blocks and boards), signs and labels
Ask parents if have and will loan	potted plants; clipboards	butterfly collection, cash register
Characters	eggs, butterflies, caterpillars, chrysalises, birds, toads, people	cashier, guide, guard, curator, visitor, store manager, suppliers
Things to do	Walk through habitat. Be one of animals. Be a visitor looking at butterflies. Be a lepidopterist.	Visit museum. Give a tour. Guard museum. Choose and arrange displays. Buy or sell things at gift shop. Sell things to museum.

See the **Art** section (Life Cycle; Butterflies) for ideas for puppets, costumes, and murals.

- After reading the Big Book, *The Longest Journey in the World* by William Barrett Morris, help students act out the story. Ask the students what objects the caterpillar crawled on during its journey. If possible, gather the actual objects (hose, flowerpot, rake, etc.), or use props drawn by the children. Arrange the objects in the order they were encountered. Have students recreate the journey as they retell the story.

- After reading *The Very Hungry Caterpillar* by Eric Carle, act out the story. Make a list of the food the caterpillar eats. Have the students draw and paint the food on paper or cardboard. Place the foods in the sequence found in the story. As the children act out the story, they can pretend to nibble the food.

- Make felt board characters to act out the butterfly life cycle, or to dramatize butterfly stories students have heard or have created.

- Children can use puppets to act out their own plays or published plays. Readers Theatre, chants, poems, finger plays, and songs can also come alive with puppetry. Puppets can be made from many different materials. Students can make simple finger puppets, hand puppets, glove puppets, and stick puppets. Suggestions are provided in the **Art** section (Life Cycle). See the **Language Arts** and **Music** sections for literature and songs.

- Prepare and present a butterfly performance. Invite other classes and/or parents to hear children sing songs, perform butterfly chants, poems, and Readers Theatre, reenact favorite stories, and present their own skits. Ideas for skits about butterfly conservation are offered in the Social Studies section.

- Explore butterfly and caterpillar behaviors through creative movement. Have students act out some of the following actions.

Be a butterfly egg: *(child can curl up, hiding head)*
   being very still
Be a caterpillar: *(child can hold arms at sides or tuck arms inside shirt)*
   wiggling in an egg
   nibbling a hole in the egg
   crawling out of the egg
   munching on a leaf
   hiding from a bird
   playing dead
   sticking out your osmeterium (swallowtail)
   molting
   becoming a chrysalis

Be a chrysalis: *(child can put hands together over head and pretend to hang from an object)*
   stabbing cremaster into silk pad
   wiggling and gyrating as a newly formed chrysalis
   hanging motionless

Be a butterfly: *(child can flutter arms or wave scarves)*
   hatching from a chrysalis
   grabbing onto a branch
   pumping wings full of blood
   drying wings
   tasting food *(use your feet)*
   flying *(different butterfly flight patterns including darting, sailing gently, bobbing frenetically, zipping up and down, making tiny circles, etc.)*
   at rest *(wings over head)*
   sipping nectar

Suggestions for forming a cooperative large moving caterpillar are offered in the **Physical Activities** section.

MUSIC

Experiences with songs and rhythms can help children grow in many ways. The experiences in this section stress the fun and joy of music, and help children develop a greater sense of community with their peers. The songs also help the children to learn new information about butterflies, use new language patterns and vocabulary, and develop their musical listening skills.

Music and language arts are easily integrated. The words to a song can be written on a chart or transparency for reading. New verses written by the group can become further material for reading and singing. Different song patterns can be explored (e.g. cumulative ones, ones with choral refrains) and students may be motivated to compose their own songs using some of these patterns.

The songs in this section are original words set to familiar tunes.

Experiences

- Write the words to the songs on large charts or make a transparency of the text to use on the overhead projector.

- Model the song by singing and pointing to the text. Invite students to join in.

- Add rhythm instruments and body movements to bring new dimensions to the performance of a piece.

- Together, the class can create additional verses, or create lyrics of their own to favorite tunes.

- Make favorite songs into Sing-Along Big Books. Write part of the song on each page. The class can provide illustrations for each line, pair of lines, or verse.

- Make tape recordings of the singing. The class can sing along with their own repertoire of songs on tape.

I'm a Little Caterpillar

(to the tune of "I'm a Little Teapot")
SCIENCE CONCEPT 2: Metamorphosis

> I'm a little caterpillar
> round and fat.
> Here is my body,
> Here are my legs.
> When I've finished molting
> Then I'll shout
> I'm in a chrysalis
> Let me out!

MUSIC

Metamorphosis

(to the tune of "Up on the Housetop")
SCIENCE CONCEPT 2: Metamorphosis

First comes a butterfly and lays an egg,
Out comes a caterpillar with tiny legs.
See the caterpillar shed its skin
Then a chrysalis just to sleep in.

Look, look, look, see it now.
Look, look, look, see it now.
Out of the chrysalis, my, oh, my
Out comes a graceful butterfly!

The Butterfly Dance

(to the tune of "Frère Jacques")
SCIENCE CONCEPT 3: Basic Needs

Butterflies
Butterflies,
See them twirl,
Flutter and stop.
Colorful and graceful,
Swirling in the sunshine,
Butterflies,
Butterflies.

Caterpillars

(to the tune of "Frère Jacques")
SCIENCE CONCEPT 3: Basic Needs

Caterpillars,
Caterpillars,
See them eat
A leafy treat.
Munching, crunching, munching,
Munching, crunching, munching,
Caterpillars,
Caterpillars.

Do You Know the Butterflies?

(to the tune of "Do You Know the Muffin Man?")
SCIENCE CONCEPT 5: Variety

Do you know the butterfly
The butterfly, the butterfly?
Do you know the butterfly
That's orange, black and white?

Yes, I know the butterfly,
The butterfly, the butterfly.
Yes, I know the butterfly
It is the . . . Monarch!

A-Hunting We Will Go

SCIENCE CONCEPT 5: Variety

You may want to create a chart of this song, writing the names of different caterpillars on removable labels. Children can create different verses by selecting and attaching a caterpillar name to the chart. For a more detailed description of this activity, see the **Science** *section (Concept 5: Variety).*

A-hunting we will go,
A-hunting we will go.
We'll catch ourselves
A caterpillar
And then we'll let it go!

A-hunting we will go,
A-hunting we will go.
We'll catch ourselves
A butterfly
And then we'll let it go!

(Verse) A-hunting we will go,
A-hunting we will go.
We'll catch ourselves
A Mourning Cloak
And then we'll let it go!

A-hunting we will go,
A-hunting we will go.
We'll catch ourselves
A Painted Lady
And then we'll let it go!

Little Arabella Miller

(to the tune of "Twinkle, Twinkle Little Star")

SCIENCE CONCEPT 2: Metamorphosis

Little Arabella Miller
Had a fuzzy caterpillar.
First it climbed upon her mother,
Then upon her baby brother.
They said, Arabella Miller,
Take away your caterpillar!

(wiggle fingers of one hand in palm of other)
(fingers crawl along arm to shoulder)

(shake finger at Arabella)

Little Arabella Miller
Had a fuzzy caterpillar.
First it climbed upon her mother,
Then upon her baby brother.
They said, Arabella Miller,
How we love your caterpillar!

(wiggle fingers of one hand in palm of other)
(fingers crawl along arm to shoulder)

(smile and stroke caterpillar sweetly)

Where?

(to the tune of "Where is Thumbkin?")

SCIENCE CONCEPT 2: Metamorphosis

Where is egg?
Where is egg?

Here I am
Here I am
Now I'm a caterpillar
I'm a caterpillar
That I am!
That I am!

Where is caterpillar?
Where is caterpillar?

Here I am
Here I am
Now I'm a small chrysalis
I'm a small chrysalis
That I am!
That I am!

Where is chrysalis?
Where is chrysalis?

Here I am
Here I am
Now I'm a gorgeous butterfly
I'm a gorgeous butterfly
That I am!
THAT I AM!

Winter Time

(to the tune of "Where Oh Where has My Doggie Gone?")
SCIENCE CONCEPT 3: Basic Needs

Oh where, oh where has my butterfly gone?
Oh where, oh where can he be?
It is cold outside
I'm afraid he will die
Oh where, oh where can he be?

Oh where, oh where has my Monarch gone?
Oh where, oh where can she be?
Did she migrate south
Safe from winter's chill?
Oh where, oh where can she be?

Oh where, oh where has my Swallowtail gone?
Oh where, oh where can he be?
Is he now a pupa
Safe from winter's chill?
Oh where, oh where can he be?

Oh where, oh where has my Copper gone?
Oh where, oh where can she be?
Is she now an egg
Safe from winter's chill?
Oh where, oh where can she be?

Oh where, oh where has my Admiral gone?
Oh where, oh where can he be?
Is he now a larva
Safe from winter's chill?
Oh where, oh where can he be?

Butterfly Connections

(to the tune of "Dem Bones")
SCIENCE CONCEPT 2: Metamorphosis

The head's connected to the thorax.
The thorax is connected to the forewing.
The forewing's connected to the hind wing.
The hind wing's connected to the thorax.
The thorax is connected to the abdomen.
Oh, see the butterfly fly!

The Fuzzy Caterpillar

(to the tune of "The Eensy-Weensy Spider")
SCIENCE CONCEPT 2: Metamorphosis

The fuzzy caterpillar
Crawled up the garden vine,
Came to a green leaf
and there it stopped to dine.
Soon it was a chrysalis
dreaming it could fly.
Later when it woke up
It was a butterfly!

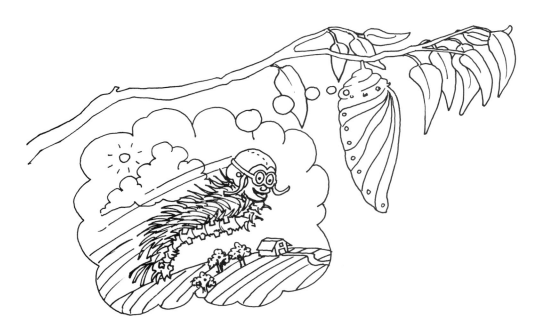

Oh, See the Caterpillar Train

(to the tune of "Dem Bones")

SCIENCE CONCEPT 2: Metamorphosis

The head's connected to the first segment.
The first segment's connected to the second segment.
The second segment's connected to the third segment.

Chorus: Oh, see the caterpillar train!

The third segment's connected to the fourth segment.
The fourth segment's connected to the fifth segment.
The fifth segment's connected to the sixth segment.

Chorus: Oh, see the caterpillar train!

The sixth segment's connected to the seventh segment.
The seventh segment's connected to the eighth segment.
The eighth segment's connected to the ninth segment.

Chorus: Oh, see the caterpillar train!

The ninth segment's connected to the tenth segment.
The tenth segment's connected to the eleventh segment.
The eleventh segment's connected to the twelfth segment.

Chorus: Oh, see the caterpillar train!

The twelfth segment's connected to the thirteenth segment.
The thirteenth segment's connected to the fourteenth segment.
The fourteenth segment is the caboose.

Chorus: Oh, see the caterpillar train!

Published Music

In addition to the songs printed above, we have also enjoyed published and recorded butterfly music with our students. We recommend the following pieces:

"Arabella Miller," "Mr. Egg," and "Butterfly," recorded by Susan Bamel on *Sing a Song*.

"Caterpillars on the Run" and "Lovely Butterflies," by Stephen Titra in his songbook, *Be Nice to Spiders, Be Nice to Snakes*.

"The Caterpillar" by Emilie Poulsson in the songbook, *Singing Bee! A Collection of Favorite Children's Songs*, compiled by Jane Hart.

For more information, see the Bibliography.

MUSIC

NOTES

PHYSICAL ACTIVITIES

Young children are naturally active and learn about themselves and their world through physical activities. The experiences in this section provide students with opportunities to extend their knowledge of butterflies while they develop physical skills: spatial awareness, coordination, balance, agility, stamina, and strength.

Experiences

Butterfly Tag

SCIENCE CONCEPT 4: Protective Behaviors

The children are butterflies. One child is selected to be "It." That child is a butterfly predator—a bird, a lizard, or whatever that child chooses to be. The predator chases the butterflies. The butterflies call time-out by yelling "camouflage." To make the game more complicated, when a butterfly yells "camouflage" he or she must touch something that is the same color as an article of clothes he or she is wearing. Any variation of tag can be incorporated into this game.

Metamorphosis Obstacle Course

SCIENCE CONCEPTS 2 and 3: Metamorphosis; Basic Needs

Set up a metamorphosis obstacle course on the playground. The children can perform specific tasks at different stations. For example, the children can sit like an egg in one spot, crawl like a caterpillar through and over things in another, hang like a chrysalis elsewhere, and then fly like a butterfly to the nectar (perhaps a dandelion). Children can label the course with signs indicating the place and the required activity.

Cooperative Caterpillar Crawl

SCIENCE CONCEPT 2: Metamorphosis

A small group, which can gradually expand, can form a caterpillar. Each child can form one segment of the caterpillar: the head, thorax, and abdomen, etc. Have children get on their hands and knees and hold onto the ankles or the waist of the child in front of them. The cooperative caterpillar can crawl around the room, going under tables, over blocks, around chairs, out the door, etc.

This activity is fun to do in conjunction with the song "See the Caterpillar Train." See the **Music** section.

Field Trips

ALL CONCEPTS

Children can go on field trips to count butterflies (see the **Math** section); find larval food; observe or collect eggs, caterpillars, chrysalises, and butterflies in their natural habitats; discover different habitats of different species; and observe destruction of habitats.

Fluttering Butterflies

SCIENCE CONCEPT 2: Metamorphosis

Begin by playing music appropriate to the flight patterns of different butterflies. The children can start as chrysalises and slowly emerge as butterflies. Using scarves, they can pump blood into their wings and then flutter about.

NOTES

COOKING

Anatomical features and the variety of caterpillars and butterflies can be playfully explored in these cooking experiences. Cooking will also provide children with opportunities to read directions, measure and count ingredients, tell time, observe the changes in ingredients as they are combined and heated, and to enjoy something to eat! Many of these cooking experiences may be appropriate in preparation for a class celebration at the conclusion of the study of butterflies.

Experiences

Nectar

This recipe is not really nectar, but if students use their imagination they can pretend they are a butterfly sipping nectar.

Measure and mix together:

> 1 can frozen lime or lemon juice
> 1 can water
> 2 cups ginger ale
> 2 tablespoons honey
> a tray of ice

Serve with straws, so the nectar can be sucked through a proboscis!

Butterfly Toast

Using a butterfly-shaped cookie cutter or a cardboard template, cut butterfly shapes from slices of bread. Toast the bread and then cover it with a sticky substance such as honey or peanut butter. Decorate the butterfly wings with raisins, cereal, candy sprinkles or any item which simulates scales.

Stained Glass Butterfly Cookies

Make a dough from a simple butter cookie recipe. Chill and roll the dough approximately 1/8 inch thick. Cut out butterfly-shaped cookies with a cookie cutter or with a knife tracing around a butterfly stencil. Scoop or cut dough out from the center section of each wing. Line the cookie sheet with aluminum foil. Grease the foil. Place the butterfly cookies on the foil. Fill the holes in the wings with crushed hard candy.

Caterpillars On a Leaf

Mix together:

> 1 cup peanut butter
> 1 cup honey
> 1 cup dry milk
> 1/2 cup wheat germ

Give each child a heaping tablespoon of the mixture to shape into a caterpillar. The "caterpillar" can be rolled in sesame seeds, be decorated with patterns of cereal bits, raisins, etc. Serve the "caterpillar" on a lettuce leaf.

Marshmallow Caterpillars

Paint marshmallows with a "paint" made of a few drops of food coloring in 1/4 cup of milk. This paint will add color and help the marshmallows stick together. While the marshmallows are still wet, stick them together and place on a piece of wax paper. If a stronger glue appears to be needed, use the following recipe to make frosting cement.

Frosting Cement

   2 egg whites
   1/2 tsp. cream of tartar
   2 cups confectioners sugar

Beat the egg whites until stiff. Add cream of tartar. Then add two cups of sugar. With an electric mixer beat the mixture for approximately three minutes. Using the cement as a glue, decorate the caterpillar with raisins, peanuts, chocolate chips, etc. for eyes, feet, spots, projections, etc.

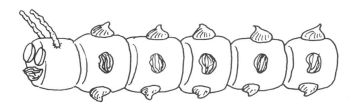

NOTES

GLOSSARY

androconia—a specialized scent scale, found on the wings of some male butterflies. The scent attracts female butterflies for mating.

antenna, plural antennae—a sense organ on the head of an insect

caterpillar—common name for the larva of a butterfly or moth

chitin (KITE-en)—the liquid produced by an insect's body which hardens and forms its exoskeleton. In the butterfly, chitin forms the outer covering of the caterpillar, the chrysalis, and the surface under the scales on both sides of the butterfly's wing.

chrysalis (KRISS-uh-lis), plural chrysalises or chrysalids—pupa of the butterfly

cremaster (kree-MAS-ter)—a hooklike process on the end of a chrysalis that attaches the pupa to a stem, twig, etc.

crochets (kro-SHAYS)—hooks found on the ends of prolegs of a caterpillar

entomologist—a scientist who studies insects

exuvia (ig-ZOO-vee-ah)—the molted skin of a caterpillar or any other animal

frass—the droppings of a caterpillar

habitat—the place where an animal lives

instar—the period between two larval (caterpillar) molts

larva, plural larvae—the second stage of metamorphosis in which the insect has no wings and is wormlike

lepidoptera—name of the order to which butterflies belong

mandibles—the jaws or mouth parts of a caterpillar

metamorphosis (met-uh-MOR-fuh-sis)—the series of developmental stages through which insects go to become adults. Through metamorphosis a butterfly is transformed from an egg, to a caterpillar, to a chrysalis, to a butterfly.

molting—shedding of the exoskeleton or skin during growth to make way for a new skin

mimicry—the resemblance of one individual to another object, usually aiding in concealment or protection

nectar—a sweet substance produced by flowers that butterflies use as food

ocelli—simple eyes of some insects. Caterpillars have ten to twelve ocelli.

osmeterium (oz-meh-TER-ee-um)—a Y-shaped retractable organ near the head of a swallowtail caterpillar. When erect, it gives off an unpleasant odor.

proboscis (pro-BAHS-kiss)—the long feeding tube coiled under the head of the adult butterfly. When extended it is used to suck nectar and water.

pupa (PEW-puh), plural pupae (PEW-pee)—the third stage of the metamorphosis, the chrysalis

pupate—to change from a caterpillar (larva) to a chrysalis (pupa)

scales—highly modified flattened hairs which form the hard shinglelike covering on the membrane of the wing

spinneret—the tube through which silk emerges from a caterpillar's body

spiracles—respiratory (breathing) openings on an insect's body. Found on the caterpillar, chrysalis, and butterfly.

thorax—the middle portion of an insect's body that bears the legs and wings

veins—tubelike structures that give strength to the wings and allow for the flow of butterfly's blood (hemolymph)

BIBLIOGRAPHY

The Bibliography has been divided into the following categories:
**Fiction, Nonfiction, Big Books, Magazine Articles, Poetry, Field Guides
and Other Reference Books, Whole-Language Resources, Theme Study
Resources, Music, Filmstrips and Videos, Posters, Butterfly Stickers.**

FICTION

Aldridge, Alan. *The Butterfly Ball and the Grasshopper's Feast*. New York: Grossman Pub., 1975.
This story written in rhyme is based on William Roscoe's "The Butterfly Ball and the Grass-hopper's Feast." Various creatures (gadfly, dormouse, mole, hare . . .) prepare for the Butterfly's ball.

Brown, Ruth. *If At First You Do Not See*. New York: Holt, Rinehart and Winston, 1983.
A caterpillar has a frightful trip as it wanders in search of food. The writing wraps around the sides of the illustrations and each picture held upside down reveals a second surprise image.

Broger, Achim. *The Caterpillar's Story*. New York: Scroll Press, Inc., 1971.
The story of the metamorphosis of a butterfly, told by a caterpillar who wishes it could fly.

Butterworth, Nick. *Amanda's Butterfly*. New York: Delacorte Press, 1991.
This wordless picture book tells the story of a young girl who tries to catch a butterfly. When it starts to rain, the girl takes shelter in a garden shed where she encounters a wonderful surprise.

Caduto, Michael J. and Joseph Bruchac. "How the Butterflies Came to Be" in *Keepers of the Animals: Native American Stories and Wildlife Activities for Children*. Golden, CO: Fulcrum Pub., 1991.
A Southwest Native American Indian (Papago) pourquoi story.

Carle, Eric. *The Very Busy Spider*. New York: Philomel Books, 1984.
Children can use the structure of this story to create a Readers' Theater about a very busy butterfly.

_____. *The Very Hungry Caterpillar*. New York: Philomel Books, 1979.
A beautifully illustrated text that engages young readers through its repetitive refrain. On each day of the week the caterpillar eats a range of delights until it eats through a leaf, forms a chrysalis, and later emerges as a beautiful butterfly. Also available as a Big Book and as a paperback from Scholastic.

Conklin, Gladys,. *I Like Caterpillars*. New York: Holiday, 1958.
A young child delights in learning about caterpillars. Drawings show a wide variety of caterpillars; an identification key is provided at the end.

_____. *I Like Butterflies*. New York: Holiday, 1960.
A sequel to *I Like Caterpillars*, this book features similar content and format.

Delaney, Ned. *One Dragon to Another*. Boston: Houghton Mifflin Co., 1976.
A caterpillar and a dragon learn to appreciate their differences in this easy-to-read story of friendship. Fanciful, bold drawings make this an engaging text.

DeLuise, Dom. *Charlie the Caterpillar*. New York: Simon and Schuster, 1990.
The other animals call Charlie the Caterpillar "ugly" and turn him away, then when he emerges as a beautiful butterfly they all want him to be their friend. But Charlie flies away to find happiness with a true friend.

First Graders of A.R. Shepherd School. *A Caterpillar's Wish*. Worthington, OH: Willowisp Press, Inc., 1988.
A story about a ladybug and a caterpillar, told and illustrated by a group of first-grade students.

Garelick, May. *Where Do Butterflies Go When It Rains?* Reading, MA: Addison-Wesley, 1961.
With a lovely repetitive pattern and a poetic text, the author engages young readers in thinking about what various insects and other animals do when it rains.

Gomi, Taro. *Hi Butterfly.* New York: William Morrow, 1983.
With bold, simple illustrations and a few words, this book recounts the adventures of a little boy who tries to catch a butterfly.

Grifalconi, Ann. *Darkness and the Butterfly.* Boston: Little Brown and Co., 1987.
Osa, a young African girl, fearless during the day becomes afraid at night. A wise woman helps her overcome her fear by telling her a parable about the butterfly.

Hines, Anna Grossnickle. *Remember the Butterflies.* New York: Dutton Children's Books, 1991.
Two children learn to accept the loss of a beautiful butterfly through the guidance and support of their nature-loving grandfather. This prepares them for a later, more difficult loss.

Hobart, Ann. *A New Friend for Morganfield.* Portland, ME: Guy Gannett Pub. Co., 1985.
A story about the development of Monarch butterflies in Maine as told through the eyes of a friendly mouse. Includes an epilogue of factual information.

Howe, James. *I Wish I Were a Butterfly.* San Diego: Harcourt Brace Jovanovich, 1987.
A cricket thinks he's ugly until a spider and a butterfly help him see things differently. Ed Young's magnificent watercolors complement the delicate language of this tale.

Kent, Jack. *The Caterpillar and the Polliwog.* New York: Prentice-Hall, Inc., 1982.
A comical story of a caterpillar who boasts she will turn into something else when she grows up. Her admiring audience, a polliwog, wistfully wishes that he too could change.

Lester, Julius. "How God Made the Butterflies" in *Black Folktales.* New York: Richard W. Baron, 1969.
An African-American pourquoi story.

Lieberherr-Kubler, Ruth. *The Caterpillar and the Butterfly.* Scharer and Muller, 1985.
A simple story about a caterpillar who experiences metamorphosis and befriends other insects including, finally, another butterfly.

Morris, William Barrett. *The Longest Journey in the World.* New York: Holt, Rinehart and Winston, 1982.
This story of a caterpillar's amazing journey invites children to explore the sense of relative size. Also available as a Big Book and on audiocassette (Holt, Rinehart and Winston).

O'Gorman, Ned. *The Blue Butterfly.* New York: Harper and Row, 1971.
This tale describes the journey of a blue butterfly and the experience of the boy traveling with him.

Philip, Neil, ed. "The Spring Butterflies" in *The Spring of Butterflies and other Folktales of China's Minority Peoples.* New York: Lothrop, Lee and Shepard, 1985.

Politi, Leo. *The Butterflies Come.* New York: Charles Scribner's Sons, 1957.
Two children in California learn about Monarch migration after they see a cloud of butterflies.

Pugh, Ellen. "The Three Butterflies" in *More Tales From the Welsh Hills.* New York: Dodd, Mead and Co., 1971.

Rockwell, Anne and Harlow. *Sally's Caterpillar.* New York: Parents' Magazine Press. 1966.
This is the story of a young girl who raises a caterpillar.

Selsam, Millicent E. *Terry and the Caterpillars.* New York: Harper and Row, 1962.
An easy, "I can read" science book about a young lepidopterist, featuring a clear, simple description of the life cycle of the Cecropia moth.

Sundgaard, Arnold. *The Lamb and the Butterfly.* New York: Orchard Books, 1988.
A poetic and rhythmic text about a lamb and a butterfly who learn about each other's life. Eric Carle's exquisite collages make this book particularly appealing to young children.

Wiest, Robert and Claire. *Down the River Without a Paddle*. Chicago: Children's Press, 1973.
The exciting story of a caterpillar who travels down a river on a leaf. The watercolor illustrations provide a wonderful model for children's own paintings in response to the story.

Williams, Karen Lynn. *Baseball and Butterflies*. New York: Lothrop, Lee and Shepard, 1990.
A chapter book about a third-grader who is fascinated by butterflies. His summer butterfly project is endangered by his younger brother and by his baseball-playing friends.

Yolen, Jane. *An Invitation to the Butterfly Ball: A Counting Rhyme*. New York: Parents' Magazine Press, 1976.
A succession of animals, from one little mouse to ten little porcupines, prepare to attend the Butterfly Ball. An engaging cumulative tale for reading aloud or for shared reading.

Yoshi. *The Butterfly Hunt*. Saxonville, MA: Picture Book Studio, 1990.
A story of a young butterfly hunter told in few words and with wonderfully expressive pictures. The conclusion conveys an important message to young nature lovers.

NONFICTION

For listings of nonfiction books about specific butterfly species, refer to Concept 5 in the Science section.

Braithwaite, Althea. *Butterflies*. Chicago: Dearborn Financial Publishing, 1988.
Simple text and drawings describe the life cycle of a Swallowtail.

Chinery, Michael. *Butterfly*. Mahwah, NJ: Troll Associates, 1991.
Photographs and drawings illustrate the life cycle of a Swallowtail butterfly.

Cole, Joanna. *An Insect's Body*. New York: William Morrow and Co., 1984.
The characteristics of an insect are described, using a cricket as an example. Diagrams and black-and-white photographs.

Cutts, David. *Look ... A Butterfly*. Mahwah, NJ: Troll Associates, 1982.
Beautifully illustrated book about the life cycle of a butterfly. Simple text.

Dallinger, Jane and Cynthia Overbeck. *Swallowtail Butterflies*. Minneapolis: Lerner Publications Co., 1982.
Vivid photographs and a rich informative text describe the Swallowtail butterfly in all the stages of development. Includes information about feeding, reproduction, and survival of butterflies in various parts of the world. Appropriate for intermediate readers or as a teacher reference.

Drew, David. *Caterpillar Diary*. Crystal Lake, IL: Rigby Inc., 1987.
A magnificent Big Book filled with information and wonderful close-up photographs depicting the life of a Emperor Gum Moth caterpillar. Charts, diagrams, and a useful index. Suitable for all ages. Available in small book size; a wall chart is also available.

_____. *The Life of the Butterfly*. Crystal Lake, IL: Rigby Inc., 1987.
A wonderful Big Book tracing the life cycle of a Cabbage White butterfly through close-up photographs. Interesting information is presented through varied formats. Diagrams, index and glossary. Suitable for all ages. Also available in small book size. A wall chart is also offered.

Eastman, Patricia. *Sometimes Things Change*. Chicago: Children's Press, 1983.
This easy-to-read Big Book with simple colorful illustrations describes a variety of things that become something else, including a caterpillar that changes into a butterfly.

Fischer-Nagel, Heiderose and Andreas. *Life of the Butterfly*. Minneapolis: Carolrhoda Books, Inc., 1983.
Beautiful photographs and detailed text tell the story of the Peacock butterfly and includes information on habits and behaviors of butterflies in general. Paperback edition available from First Avenue Editions, Minneapolis, Minnesota.

Florian, Douglas. *Discovering Butterflies*. New York: Charles Scribner's Sons, 1986.
This book describes the life cycle, anatomy, and behaviors of the butterfly. It includes drawings and information about a variety of butterfly species. Paperback available from Aladdin Books, New York.

Gibbons, Gail. *Monarch Butterfly*. New York: Holiday, 1989.
A simple text and large drawings describe the anatomy and behavior of the Monarch. Includes instructions on how to raise a Monarch.

Goor, Ron and Nancy. *Insect Metamorphosis*. New York: Atheneum, 1990.
Through close-up full-color photographs, the stages of development of many different insects are shown. Includes the complete metamorphosis of the Mourning Cloak butterfly and very detailed descriptions of the caterpillar stages.

Goudey, Alice E. *Butterfly Time*. New York: Charles Scribner's Sons, 1964.
In a poetic text, a young boy and girl share their observations of well-known butterflies through the seasons.

Heller, Ruth. *How to Hide a Butterfly*. New York: Grosset and Dunlap, 1985.
Wonderful drawings and simple text reveal how insects camouflage themselves.

Herberman, Ethan. *The Great Butterfly Hunt*. New York: Simon and Schuster, 1990.
This NOVA book gives an historical and personal account of how the Monarch's overwintering locations in Mexico were discovered, and examines many other aspects of Monarch studies. A lengthy and sophisticated text with photographs.

Hoffman, Don. *Wanderer: The Monarch Butterfly*. Morro Bay, CA: Natural History Association of San Luis Obispo Coast, Inc., 1989.
A lengthy and detailed text about the Monarch butterfly. Contains beautiful photographs.

Hogan, Paula Z. *The Butterfly*. Milwaukee: Raintree Children's Books, 1979.
Large colorful illustrations help tell an introductory story of the life cycle. An audiocassette is available.

Huntington, Harriet E. *Let's Look at Insects*. Garden City NY: Doubleday and Co., 1969.
This book describes the characteristics of insects. Anatomical features as well as other attributes are discussed. For older readers.

Hutchins, Ross. *The Travels of Monarch X*. New York: Rand McNally and Co., 1966.
A true story of the travels of a Monarch butterfly caught by a Mexican boy after a long hazardous flight. A fascinating account of migration written in clear, simple language.

Ivy, Bill. *Nature's Children: Monarch Butterfly*. Danbury, CT: Grolier Limited, 1985.
Large photographs and descriptive text tell of the Monarch's life cycle, migration, and other behaviors.

Josephson, Judith. *The Monarch Butterfly*. Riverside, NJ: Crestwood House, 1988.
This book is written for older readers.

Jourdan, Eveline. *Butterflies and Moths Around the World*. Minneapolis: Lerner, 1981.
This book describes the life cycle of moths and butterflies and gives information about the habits and characteristics of more than fifty species.

Kratky, Lada Josefa. *Animals and Their Young*. Carmel, CA: Hampton-Brown Books, 1991.
This Big Book is filled with interesting facts and photographs of a variety of animals and their young. It includes a beautiful description of a developing butterfly. Also available in small book size.

Lepthien, Emilie U. *Monarch Butterflies*. Chicago: Children's Press, 1989.
Beautiful photographs and large print describe the physical characteristics, migration, life cycle, and habitat needs of the Monarch. Also discusses conservation efforts.

Martin, Bill, Jr. *Butterflies Becoming*. Little Nature Books. Chicago: Encyclopedia Britannica, 1975.
Poetic text describes metamorphosis. Audiocassette available.

May, Julian. *Life Cycle of a Monarch Butterfly*. Mankato, MN: Creative Education, 1973.

Morris, Dean. *Butterflies and Moths*. Milwaukee: Raintree Children's Books, 1977.
Discusses the difference between butterflies and moths, and describes protective behaviors, life cycle, and anatomy of the different stages. Clear text and simple illustrations.

Nash, Pamela. *The Butterfly*. Cleveland: Modern Curriculum Press, 1983.
An easy-to-read text describing the life cycle of a butterfly.

Norsgaard, E. Jaediker. *How to Raise Butterflies*. New York: Dodd, Mead and Co., 1988.
This book contains beautiful photographs clearly showing the life cycles of the Monarch and the Black Swallowtail. Good source book for students interested in catching and raising butterflies.

Oda, Hidetomo. *Butterflies*. Milwaukee: Raintree, 1986.
Detailed instructions on how to raise Monarchs. The appendix lists various caterpillars, their food sources and the overwintering stage of each species.

_____. *The Swallowtail Butterfly*. Milwaukee: Raintree, 1986.

O'Hagan, Caroline. *It's Easy to Have a Caterpillar Visit You*. New York: Lothrop, Lee and Shephard, 1980.
Instructions for caring for all stages of development: catching, housing, feeding, and releasing.

Oxford Scientific Films. *The Butterfly Cycle*. New York: G. P. Putnam's Sons, 1977.
This book shows the life cycle of the Cabbage White butterfly. The large photographs are ideal for sharing close-up details with a group.

Pallotta, Jerry. *The Icky Bug Alphabet Book*. Watertown, MA: Charlesbridge Publishing, 1986.
An informative ABC book about a variety of bugs. A good model for children interested in making their own insect ABC book.

Parker, Nancy Winslow and Joan Richards Wright. *Bugs*. New York: Greenwillow, 1987.
A clever and engaging book that includes diagrams, factual information, and riddles about sixteen insects.

Podendorf, Illa. *Insects*. A New True Book. Chicago: Children's Press, 1981.
In simple text, various characteristics of insect development and behaviors are described. Clear pictures of the development of the Monarch and Cabbage butterflies.

Porter, Keith. *Discovering Butterflies and Moths*. New York: The Bookwright Press, 1986.
Describes the life cycle, daily life, use of colors, and enemies of the butterfly and moth. Contains excellent photographs.

Reidel, Marlene. *From Egg to Butterfly*. Minneapolis: Carolrhoda Books, 1974.
Simple text and drawings explain the life cycle of the butterfly.

Rowan, James P. *Butterflies and Moths*. Chicago: Children's Press, 1983.
In large, easy-to-read text, the characteristics, life cycle, and the behaviors of butterflies are described. Includes information on protection, migration, and hibernation, as well as a brief glossary.

Ryder, Joanne. *Where Butterflies Grow*. New York: E.P. Dutton, 1989.
The life story of the Black Swallowtail told through poetic text. The beautiful detailed illustrations are by Lynne Cherry.

Russo, Monica. *The Insect Almanac: A Year-Round Activity Guide*. New York: Sterling Publishing Company, 1991.
This illustrated guide shows students how to find, identify, and collect butterflies and other insects. The guide contains many activities to help children learn about insects during different seasons.

Sabin, Louis. *Amazing World of Butterflies and Moths*. Mahwah, NJ: Troll Associates, 1982.
Briefly describes the life cycles of butterflies and moths. Audiocassette available.

Selsam, Millicent E. *Backyard Insects*. New York: Scholastic Book Services, 1981.
Photographs show how insects protect themselves: camouflage, warning colors, mimicry, flash coloration, and eye spots.

_____. *A First Look at Insects*. New York: Walker and Co., 1974.
A clear description of the characteristics of insects. Contains realistic, detailed drawings.

_____. *Where Do They Go? Insects in Winter*. New York: Four Winds Press, 1982.
Contains easy-to-read information on what happens to insects in winter. Drawings are accurate and colorful.

_____ and Joyce Hunt. *A First Look at Caterpillars*. New York: Walker and Co., 1987.
Describes the anatomy of the caterpillar and what features to look for when trying to identify caterpillars. A good introduction to the topic.

Spooner, Sally. *How to Raise the Monarch Butterfly*. Lakeville, MA: Spooner and Thompson, 1987.
A teacher's manual is available.

Sterling, D. *Caterpillars*. New York: Doubleday and Co., Inc., 1961.
The story of caterpillars from eggs to butterflies. Simple drawings with intriguing factual material.

Still, John. *Amazing Butterflies & Moths*. An Eyewitness Junior Book. New York: Alfred A. Knopf, Inc., 1991.
A photographic guide that illustrates the life cycle, characteristics, and behaviors of various butterflies and moths.

Walker, Colin. *Going to Be a Butterfly*. A Sunshine Book. San Diego: The Wright Group.
Easy-to-read description of the life cycle of a Monarch.

Watts, Barrie. *Butterfly and Caterpillar*. Englewood Cliffs, NJ: Silver Burdett, 1985.
Exquisite photographs and clear simple text describe the development of a Cabbage White butterfly.

_____. *Butterflies and Moths*. Keeping Minibeasts. New York: Franklin Watts, 1991.
This book contains photographs and simple instructions on how to collect, house, feed, mate, and release butterflies and moths.

_____. *Caterpillars*. New York: Franklin Watts, 1989.
The text discusses how to collect, house, and feed caterpillars, and describes their life cycle.

Whalley, Paul. *Butterfly and Moth*. Eyewitness Books. New York: Alfred A. Knopf, 1988.
The beautiful pictures in this book will fascinate young children. The text is for older readers and can also be useful as a teacher resource.

Whalley, Paul and Mary. *The Butterfly in the Garden*. Milwaukee: Gareth Stevens Publishing, 1987.
A sophisticated text illustrated with photographs, discusses the life cycle, behaviors, and adaptations of the butterfly.

BIG BOOKS

Available Big Books titles are listed here for reference. For annotations, please refer to the entry under Fiction or Nonfiction.

Carle, Eric. *The Very Hungry Caterpillar*. New York: Scholastic, 1989.

Drew, David. *Caterpillar Diary*. Crystal Lake, IL: Rigby Inc., 1987.

_____. *The Life of the Butterfly*. Crystal Lake, IL: Rigby Inc., 1987.

Eastman, Patricia. *Sometimes Things Change*. Chicago: Children's Press, 1983.

Kratky, Lada Josefa. *Animals and Their Young*. Carmel, CA: Hampton-Brown Books, 1991.

Morris, William Barrett. *The Longest Journey in the World*. New York: Holt, Rinehart and Winston, 1982.

MAGAZINE ARTICLES

Sandved, Kjell B. "Butterfly ABC." *Sesame Street Magazine*, Jan–Feb 1991: pages 16–17.

Shaver, Elizabeth. "Grow Your Own Butterfly." *Cricket*, July 1991: pages 26–28.

Thomae, Edmundo, Jr. "My Mexican Monarchs." *Ranger Rick*, Oct. 1991: pages 2–9.

POETRY

Bill Martin Jr.'s Treasury Chest of Poetry. Selected by Bill Martin, Jr. Allen, TX: DLM, 1986.
   "Ten Little Caterpillars" by Bill Martin, Jr.

Eric Carle's Animals Animals. Selected by Eric Carle. New York: Scholastic, 1989.
   "Butterflies dancing through falling snow . . . " by Demaru
   "Every Insect" by Dorothy Aldis
   "Giraffes" by Mary Ann Hoberman
   "My Opinion" by Monica Shannon

Fisher, Aileen. *Cricket in the Thicket*. New York: Charles Scribner's Sons, 1983.
   "Caterpillars"

_____. *In the Woods, In the Meadow, In the Sky*. New York: Charles Scribner's Sons, 1965.
   "Butterfly Wings"
   "Butterfly Tongues"

_____. *Inside a Little House*. New York: Robert McBride and Co., 1938.
   "Cocoons"

_____. *Out in the Dark and Daylight*. New York: Harper and Row, 1980.
   "Twice Born"

_____. *When It Comes to Bugs*. New York: Harper and Row, 1986.
   "About Caterpillars"

Fleischman, Paul. *Joyful Noise*. New York: Harper and Row, 1988.
   "Chrysalis Diary"

Finger Play Poems and Stories. Darien, CT: Teachers Publishing Corp., 1968.
   "Caterpillar, Caterpillar" by Helen Jill Fletcher

Jacobs, Leland. *Just Around the Corner*. New York: Holt, Rinehart and Winston, 1964.
   "Butterflies"

McCord, David. *All Small*. Boston: Little Brown and Co., 1986.
   "Cocoon"

Merriam, Eve. *Fresh Paint*. New York: Macmillian Publishing Co., 1986.
   "Butterflies"

Moore, Lilian. *Something New Begins*. New York: Atheneum, 1982.
   "Message from a Caterpillar"

Poetry Place Anthology. New York: Instructor Books, 1983.
   "The Cocoon" by Ethel Jacobson
   "The Insects' World" by Ethel Jacobson

Prelutsky, Jack. *Beneath A Blue Umbrella*. New York: Greenwillow Books, 1990.
   "Polly saw a butterfly . . . "
   "Patter Pitter Caterpillar . . . "

Rainbow in the Sky. Edited by Louis Untermeyer. New York: Harcourt, Brace and World, Inc., 1963.
  "The Butterfly and the Caterpillar" by Joseph Lauren

The Random House Book of Poetry for Children. Selected by Jack Prelutsky. New York: Random House, 1983.
  "Children, Children Everywhere" by Jack Prelutsky
  "Mice" by Rose Fyleman
  "The Tickle Rhyme" by Ian Serrailier

Read-Aloud Rhymes for The Very Young. Selected by Jack Prelutsky. New York: Alfred A. Knopf, 1986.
  "The Butterfly" by Clinton Scollard
  "Fuzzy Wuzzy, Creepy Crawly" by Lillian Schulz
  "Mice" by Rose Fyleman
  "Only My Opinion" by Monica Shannon

Sing a Song of Popcorn. New York: Scholastic, 1988.
  "Mice" by Rose Fyleman

Surprises. Compiled by L. B. Hopkins. New York: Harper and Row, 1984.
  "Caterpillars" by Aileen Fisher

Yolen, Jane. *Dragon Night and Other Lullabies*. New York: Methuen, 1981.
  "Caterpillar's Lullaby"

FIELD GUIDES AND OTHER REFERENCE BOOKS

Many of these reference books can be ordered through distributors specializing in butterfly materials. For specifics, refer to the listings in Appendix C: Distributors.

The Audubon Society Pocket Guides. *Familiar Butterflies: North America*. New York: Alfred A. Knopf, 1990.
  Contains 4" x 6" photographs and descriptions of the most numerous and widespread butterflies in North America. The descriptions include appropriate habitat, range, and life cycle information. The photographs are superb.

The Audubon Society Pocket Guides. *Familiar Insects and Spiders: North America*. New York: Alfred A. Knopf, 1988.
  Contains photographs and descriptions of familiar insects, using the same format as the *Familiar Butterflies* guide described above.

Brewer, Jo. "Butterfly Gardening." *Xerces Society Help Sheet 7*. (1982) 1:12.
  Order from: Xerces Society, 10 Southwest Ash Street, Portland, OR 97204.

Daccordi, Mauro, Paolo Triberti, and Andiano Zanetti. *Simon and Schuster's Guide to Butterflies and Moths*. New York: Simon and Schuster, 1987.
  This guide contains very technical information and has 300 beautiful pictures of butterflies and moths, as well as some of caterpillars. An excellent guide for viewing the variety of lepidoptera worldwide.

Damrosh, Barbara. "A Butterfly Garden." in *Theme Gardens*. New York: Workman Publishing Co., 1982.

Forey, Pamela and Cecilia Fitzsimmons. *An Instant Guide to Butterflies*. New York: Bonanza Books, 1987.
  An easy to use guide to common butterflies of North America grouped by color. Each page contains a drawing and description of the butterfly, and larva (if applicable), a distribution map, and information on habitat and larva and butterfly food source.

Hickman, Pamela M. *Bug Wise*. Reading, MA: Addison-Wesley, 1991.
  Contains information about insects and spiders and suggests related activities for children.

Howe, William. *The Butterflies of North America*. New York: Doubleday, 1975.

Klots, A. B. *A Field Guide to the Butterflies*. Boston: Houghton Mifflin Co., 1951.
An adult reference that provides intricate detail on how to identify butterflies found east of the Great Plains from Greenland to Mexico. Complete with paintings and photographs of the species, it tells about the habits, the range, the food, and habitats in which each may be found.

Mitchell, Robert T. and Herbert S. Zim. *Butterflies and Moths*. A Golden Guide. New York: Golden Press, 1962.
Contains accurate illustrations of 423 North American butterflies and moths, and some larva and pupae, grouped by families. Gives information about each family and butterfly listed, including larval food source and range maps.

Pyle, Robert Michael. *The Audubon Society Handbook for Butterfly Watchers*. New York: Charles Scribner's Sons, 1984.
This is an adult reference book covering a wide range of topics: watching, locating, counting, identifying, and rearing butterflies. Also included is butterfly gardening and conservation, and butterfly photography.

_____. *The Audubon Society Field Guide to the North American Butterflies*. New York: Alfred A. Knopf, 1981.
A useful pocket guide filled with well-organized factual material and magnificent photographs.

Stokes, Lillian and Donald, and Ernest Williams. *The Butterfly Book*. Boston: Little Brown and Co., 1991.
This book, with beautiful photographs, easy-to-read charts, and well-arranged text, contains information on metamorphosis, behavior, larval and adult food sources, habitats, broods, and gardening. An excellent source for information on common butterflies. Although the text is lengthy and sophisticated, the charts could be used by children gathering information for reports.

Tekulsky, Matthew. *Butterfly Garden*. Boston: Harvard Common Press, 1985.
This book for adults guides the reader through the whys and hows of butterfly gardening. The appendices contain valuable information on 50 butterflies, nectar sources, when to buy plants, butterflies, butterfly organizations, and a list of books to read.

Tilden, J. W. and Arthur C. Smith. *A Field Guide to Western Butterflies*. Boston: Houghton Mifflin Co., 1986.

WHOLE-LANGUAGE RESOURCES

Altwerger, B., B. Flores, and C. Edelsky. *Whole Language: What's the Difference?* Portsmouth, NH: Heinemann, 1990.

Cambourne, Brian. *The Whole Story: Natural Learning and the Acquisition of Literacy in the Classroom*. New York: Scholastic, 1980.

Goodman, Kenneth. *What's Whole in Whole Language?* Portsmouth, NH: Heinemann, 1986.

Goodman, Kenneth, L. Bird, and Y. Goodman. *The Whole Language Catalog*. Santa Rosa, CA: American School Publishers, 1991.

Holdaway, Donald. *The Foundations of Literacy*. New York: Scholastic, 1979.

Weaver, Constance. *Understanding Whole Language*. Portsmouth, NH: Heinemann, 1991.

THEME STUDY RESOURCES

Gamberg, Ruth et al. *Learning and Loving It*. Portsmouth, NH: Heineman, 1988.

Katz, Lillian G. and Sylvia C. Chard. *Engaging Children's Minds: The Project Approach*. Norwood, NJ: Ablex, 1989.

MUSIC

Bamel, Susan. *May There Always Be Sunshine.*
　　This audiocassette includes: "Butterfly," "Arabella Miller," and "Mr. Egg." Order from: Sunshine Music, 38 Bennington Street, Needham, MA 02194.

Titra, Stephen. *Be Nice to Spiders, Be Nice to Snakes.* Northbrook, IL: Hubbard Press,
　　This songbook includes: "Caterpillars on the Run" and "Lovely Butterflies." Order from: Hubbard Press, 2855 Shermer Road, Northbrook, IL 60062.

Hart, Jane (compiler). *Singing Bee! A Collection of Favorite Children's Songs.* New York: Lothrop, Lee and Shepard Books, 1982.
　　This songbook includes: "The Caterpillar" by Emilie Poulsson, set to music by Cornelia Roeske.

FILMSTRIPS AND VIDEOS

"The Life Cycle of the Monarch Butterfly"
　　This filmstrip may be ordered from: Society for Visual Education, Inc. 1345 Diversey Parkway, Chicago, IL 60614.

"The Painted Lady Butterfly"
　　Available from Connecticut Biological Supply. See Appendix C: Distributors for address and phone number.

"Baboons, Butterflies and Me"
　　This sing-along, dance-along video features Maria Muldaur and Friends. Children learn about various animals by watching the animals on film, imitating their movements in dance and finger plays, and singing songs. There is a short butterfly segment which has a song about a Swallowtail with movement and finger play. Order from: The Nature Company, P.O. Box 2310, Berkeley, CA 94702.

"Pretty Insects"
　　This video contains information about butterfly and moth habitats, behaviors, and life cycles. Order from Insect Lore. See Appendix C: Distributors for address and phone number.

POSTERS

"Butterflies Poster"
　　Poster by American Teaching Aids includes many butterfly species. Order from Papillon. See Appendix C: Distributors for address and phone number.

"Butterflies and Their Flowers"
　　A Smithsonian Institute poster. Beautiful drawings show butterflies on their preferred nectar sources. Can be ordered from Papillon or Carolina Biological Supply. See Appendix C: Distributors for addresses and phone numbers.

"Butterfly Alphabet Poster"
　　Letters of the alphabet found in the designs of butterfly wings. Beautiful close-up photographs. Order from Sundved Photography, Friendship P.O. Box 39138, Washington, DC 20016. For information call: 1-202-244-5711. To order, call: 1-800-ABC-WING.

"The Butterfly Wall Chart"
　　Eight-foot-long poster can also be used folded up, in book form. 200 butterflies are illustrated. Fact strips with location maps offer information about range, life cycles, camouflage, etc. Available from Insect Lore. See Appendix C: Distributors for address and phone number.

"Life Cycle of a Monarch"
　　A sequence chart with six panels. Order from Papillon. See Appendix C: Distributors for address and phone number.

"Painted Lady Life Cycle Poster"
   Can be ordered from Insect Lore or Carolina Biological Supply. See Appendix C: Distributors for address and phone number.

BUTTERFLY STICKERS

Grafton, Carol Belanger. *Butterfly Stickers in Full Color.* Mineola, NY: Dover Publications, 1991.
   This book contains 87 authentically detailed butterfly stickers, each portraying a different species. An excellent source for making games. It can be ordered through Papillon. See Appendix C: Distributors for address and phone number.

APPENDICES

Appendix A:
Reproducible Activity Pages and
Observation Forms

Appendix B:
Butterfly Classification Chart

Appendix C:
Distributors: (Caterpillars, chrysalises,
and related butterfly materials)

Appendix D:
Butterfly Organizations

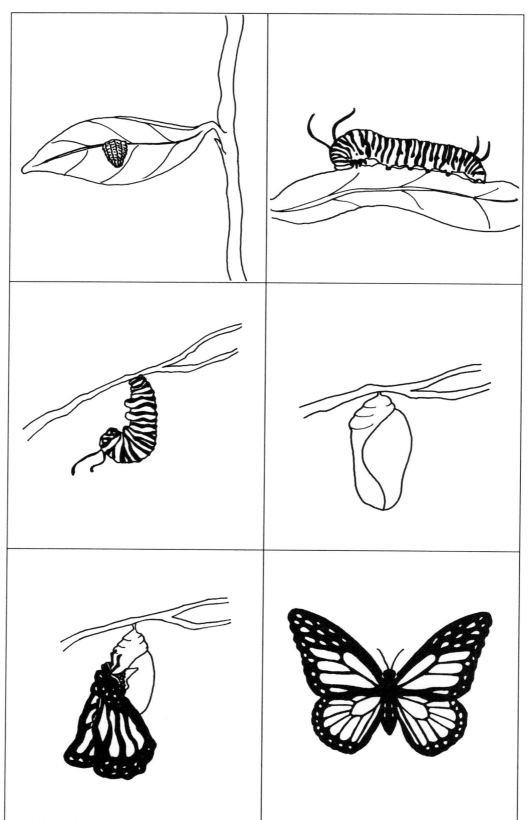

Butterfly Outline Drawings - #1

Butterfly Outline Drawings - #2

Butterfly Outline Drawings - #3

Name _____ Date _____

My Observation

APPENDICES

Name _____ Date _____

My Observation

APPENDIX B: Butterfly Classification Chart

This classification chart lists the two superfamilies, Papelionidea and Hesperioidea, the families, and the common names of some of the better-known butterflies of North America. Scientists do not always agree on how to classify butterflies. Some subfamilies on this chart will be listed as families on other charts.

PAPILIONIDEA:
"The True Butterflies"

Nymphalidae: "The Brush-footed"	Lycaenidae: Gossamer-winged	Papilionidae: "Swallowtails"	Pieridae: "Whites and Sulphurs"	Libytheinae: "Snout Butterflies"	Riodininae: "Metalmarks"
Fritillaries	Coppers	Swallowtails	Whites	Snout Butterfly	Metalmarks
Buckeyes	Blues	Spicebush	Cabbage White		
Crescents	Hairstreaks	Black			
Pearl	Elfins	Yellow	Orange Tips		
Checkerspots	Harvesters	Eastern Tiger	Sara Orange Tip		
Baltimore		Western Tiger			
Tortoise Shells		Pipevine	Sulphurs		
Mourning Cloak		Anise	Common		
Thistle Butterflies		Giant	Orange		
Painted Lady			Clouded		
West Coast Lady		Parnassians			

Fritillaries
Buckeyes
Crescents
  Pearl
Checkerspots
  Baltimore
Tortoise Shells
  Mourning Cloak
Thistle Butterflies
  Painted Lady
  West Coast Lady
  American Painted Lady
  Red Admiral
Admirals and Sisters
  White Admiral
  Viceroy
Angle Wings
  Question Mark
  Comma
"Leafwings and Emperors"
  Goatweed Butterfly
Emperor/Hackberry
Butterflies*
  Emperor
  Hackberry
Satyrs*
  Common Wood Nymphs
  Common Wood Satyr
Milkweed Butterflies*
  Monarch
  Queen
Longwing Butterflies*
  Zebra
  Julia

HESPERIOIDEA
"The Skippers"

Hesperiidae: "Skippers"	Megathymidae: "Giant Skippers"

Sometimes classified as a separate family.

APPENDIX C: Distributors

Sources for caterpillars (larva), chrysalises, and related butterfly materials.

Insect Lore Products
P.O. Box 1535
Shafter, CA 93263
805-746-6047 (customer service)
800-LIVE-BUG (orders only)

Caterpillars
Painted Lady caterpillar
Butterfly Garden (Includes: butterfly house, instructions, and coupon for three to five Painted Lady caterpillars. Caterpillars come packaged with complete food supply.)
Butterfly Garden School Kit (same as the Butterfly Garden, but includes 30 Painted Lady caterpillars.)

Books
Braithwaite, Althea. *Butterflies.*
Carle, Eric. *The Very Hungry Caterpillar.*
Fischer-Nagel, Heiderose and Andreas. *Life of the Butterfly.*
Heller, Ruth. *How to Hide a Butterfly and Other Insects.*
Mitchell, Robert and Herbert Zim. *Butterflies and Moths.* Golden Guide.
Kent, Jack. *The Caterpillar and the Polliwog.*
Pallotta, Jerry. *The Icky Bug Alphabet Book.*
Reidel, Marlene. *From Egg to Butterfly.*
Still, John. *Amazing Butterflies and Moths.* Eyewitness Junior Book.
Yoshi. *The Butterfly Hunt.*

Video
"Pretty Insects"

Posters
Painted Lady Life Cycle Poster
Butterfly Wall Chart

Puppets
Butterfly
Metamorphosis puppet: Caterpillar to Butterfly

Puzzles
Butterfly Life Cycle sequence puzzle

Papillon Distributors, Inc.
26 Bedford Street
P.O. Box 1463
Waltham, MA 02264
617-893-7875

Caterpillars and Chrysalises

Painted Lady caterpillar. (Comes in container with complete food supply. Available March–October.)
Butterfly Garden kit (Painted Lady caterpillars. For contents of kit, see listing under Insect Lore.)
Black Swallowtail chrysalis (Available all year)
Spicebush Swallowtail chrysalis (Available all year)
Tiger Swallowtail chrysalis (Available October–April)
Monarch chrysalis (Available June–September)
The Papillon Butterfly Box (Available with one or more chrysalises: choose from any of the species listed above.)

Books

The Audubon Society Pocket Guides. *Familiar Butterflies: North America.*
Forey, Pamela and Cecilia Fitzsimons. *An Instant Guide to Butterflies.*
Hoffman, Don. *Wanderer: The Monarch Butterfly.*
Mitchell, Robert and Herbert Zim. *Butterflies and Moths.* Golden Guide.
Pyle, Robert Michael. *The Audubon Society Field Guide to the North American Butterflies.*
Still, John. *Amazing Butterflies and Moths.* Eyewitness Junior Book.
Stokes, Lillian and Donald, and Ernest Williams. *The Butterfly Book.*

Posters

"Butterflies and Their Flowers"
"Butterfly Poster"

Stickers

Grafton, Carol Belanger. *Butterfly Stickers.*

Carolina Biological Supply Company
(for the Eastern U.S.)
2700 York Road
Burlington, NC 27215
919-584-0381

OR

Powell Laboratories Division
(for the Western U.S.)
Box 187
Gladstone, OR 97027
503-656-1641

Caterpillars and Chrysalises
Painted Lady caterpillar
Butterfly Garden Kit (5 Painted Lady caterpillars. See description under Insect Lore)
Swallowtail chrysalis

Books
Daccordi, Triberti and Zanetti. *Simon and Schuster's Guide to Butterflies and Moths.*
Mitchell, Robert and Herbert Zim. *Butterflies and Moths.* Golden Guide.
Pyle, Robert Michael. *The Audubon Society Field Guide to the North American Butterflies.*

Filmstrip
"The Monarch Butterfly"

Slides
Proboscis
Wing

Poster
"Butterflies and Their Flowers"

Connecticut Biological Supply Company
82 Valley Road
P.O. Box 326
Southampton, MA 01073
1-800-628-7748
413-527-4030

Caterpillars and Chrysalises
Butterfly Garden Kit (Painted Lady caterpillars. For contents of kit, see listing under Insect Lore.)
Black Swallowtail chrysalis
Eastern Tiger Swallowtail chrysalis
Spicebush Swallowtail chrysalis

Books
Herberman, Ethan. *The Great Butterfly Hunt*
Mitchell, Robert and Herbert Zim. *Butterflies and Moths.* Golden Guide.
Norsgaard, E. Jaediker. *How to Raise Butterflies*
Pyle, Robert Michael. *The Audubon Society Field Guide to the North American Butterflies.*
Tekulsky, Matthew. *Butterfly Garden*
Whalley, Paul. *Butterfly and Moth.* An Eyewitness Book.

Filmstrips
"The Painted Lady Butterfly"
"Development of Butterflies and Moths"

Poster
"Painted Lady Life Cycle Poster"

John Staples
389 Rock Beach Road
Rochester, NY 14617
716-544-8198

John Staples is a breeder of lepidoptera. He provides butterfly and moth-rearing kits featuring a choice of swallowtail species or several moth species.

APPENDIX D: Butterfly Organizations

Students can write these organizations for information about butterflies. Many cities and states have Lepidoptera clubs or entomological societies. A membership list from the Lepidopterists' Society or Xerces Society can help you locate them. If you live near a university with a zoology department or a museum with an insect collection you can seek information from them.

Entomological Society of America
9301 Annapolis Road
Lanham, MD 20706

Lepidopterists' Society
257 Common Street
Dedham, MA 02026

SASI (Sonoran Arthropod Studies, Inc.)
P.O. Box 5624
Tucson, AZ 85703

Xerces Society
10 Southwest Ash Street
Portland, OR 97204

Y.E.S. (Young Entomologists' Society)
1915 Peggy Place
Lansing, MI 48910